BUTTERFLIES
OF OKLAHOMA,
KANSAS, AND
NORTH TEXAS

BUTTERFLIES

OF OKLAHOMA,
KANSAS, AND
NORTH TEXAS

John M. Dole,
Walter B. Gerard,
and John M. Nelson

UNIVERSITY OF OKLAHOMA PRESS : NORMAN

Library of Congress Cataloging-in-Publication Data

Dole, John M.
    Butterflies of Oklahoma, Kansas, and North Texas / by John M.
    Dole, Walter B. Gerard, and John M. Nelson.
        p. cm.
    Includes bibliographical references (p.).
    ISBN 0-8061-3554-9 (pbk.: alk. paper)
    1. Butterflies—Oklahoma—Identification. 2. Butterflies—Kansas—
Identification. 3. Butterflies—Texas—Identification. 4. Butterfly
attracting—Oklahoma 5. Butterfly attracting—Kansas. 6. Butterfly
attracting—Texas. I. Gerard, Walter B., 1938– II. Nelson, John M.,
1933– III. Title.

QL551.K2D65 2004
595.78'9'09766—dc21   2003044796

BOOK DESIGN BY ELLEN BEELER

Contents

Figures and Tables

Preface

Butterflies are among earth's most delicate animals as they glide and flutter low among the plants or high in the air overhead. Their beautiful colors and thin wings add to their air of fragility. Yet butterflies are hardy creatures that endure a broad range of weather conditions, diseases, predators, and other hazards, some man-made. We hope this book will help you to enjoy the breathtaking array of butterflies in Kansas, Oklahoma, and North Texas; to identify the common species; and to join others in protecting them. We love butterflies and all that they represent, and we are confident that on closer acquaintance, you will too.

Of the approximately 255 butterflies species recorded in Kansas, Oklahoma, and North Texas, this book includes only the species most commonly seen. Luckily, many of our most beautiful butterflies are common, from the attention-getting Eastern Tiger Swallowtail (*Papilio glaucus*) to the striking Gulf Fritillary (*Agraulis vanillae*). We have also included four beautiful but lesser known species that are sure to become favorites if you are lucky enough to see them: Diana Fritillary (*Speyeria diana*), Regal Fritillary (*Speyeria idalia*), Baltimore Checkerspot (*Euphydryas phaeton*), and Swamp Metalmark (*Calephelis mutica*).

Several books are available to help you identify and learn about the butterflies not covered in this book. For the eastern portion of our region, *Butterflies through Binoculars: The East* (J. Glassberg, 1999) and *A Field Guide to Eastern Butterflies* (A. Opler, 1998) are useful. For the western portion of our region consult *Butterflies through Binoculars: The West* (J. Glassberg, 2001) and *A Field Guide to Western Butterflies* (A. Opler, 1999). Two books that cover all the butterflies of the continental

United States are *The Butterflies of North America* (J. A. Scott, 1986) and the *National Audubon Society Field Guide to North American Butterflies* (R. M. Pyle, 1981). More information on these books can be found in the bibliography.

For consistency in common and scientific names of butterflies, we follow the *Checklist and English Names of North American Butterflies* (2001) by the North American Butterfly Association. We used the *Index of Garden Plants* (Griffiths, 1994) and *An Annotated List of the Ferns, Fern Allies, Gymnosperms and Flowering Plants of Oklahoma* (Taylor and Taylor, 1989) as guides for plant names.

The maps for each species show the counties in which the species has been recorded as of January 2002. For most species, the maps reflect distribution accurately; however, for a few particularly common species, the low number of county records in western Oklahoma and Texas is more likely due to observers being in short supply in those areas rather than to a lack of butterflies.

We list abundance and season for each butterfly species, but be aware that both descriptors may vary greatly. Some species may be common to abundant in their preferred habitat but absent elsewhere. In addition, many species are more common in one part of the area covered than in the rest of it. For example, the abundance of the Red-banded Hairstreak (*Calycopis cecrops*) decreases from east to west, and the Gray Copper (*Lycaena dione*) becomes increasingly rare the farther south you go. Season of occurrence typically varies with the weather and may be advanced in warm years and delayed in cool years.

Most of the photographs in this book are by Walter Gerard, whose secrets for taking excellent photographs appear in the chapter Photographing Butterflies. Walter also wrote Life Stages and Raising Butterflies, Butterfly Survival, and many of the species accounts. John Nelson's introduction provides insights gained over many years as a professional lepidopterist; he reviewed all materials for accuracy and maintains the state butterfly list for Oklahoma. Professional horticulturist John Dole combines a love of gardening with an interest in butterflies. He wrote many of the species accounts, Butterfly Gardening, Butterfly Hotspots, and Identifying Butterflies, and he compiled the appendix listing butterfly species recorded in Kansas, Oklahoma, and North Texas. Of course, all of us reviewed and contributed to one another's work.

Acknowledgments

The skills of many people are required to produce a book, and we would like to thank those who assisted in large and small ways. Joann Karges, Bill Edwards, and Jim Mason provided information on great places to watch butterflies in North Texas and Kansas. Jeri McMahon and Randy Emmitt (www.rlephoto.com) graciously provided us with beautiful photographs of the Zebra Swallowtail and Diana Fritillary. We are grateful to John Buettner, graphics artist and fellow nature enthusiast, for the distribution maps and drawings. We greatly appreciate the Oklahoma Department of Wildlife Conservation, Wildlife Diversity Program, for giving the project its first boost with a grant. Of course, this book would not have been possible without the hard work of the people at University of Oklahoma Press, from Jean Hurtado, John Drayton, and Sally Antrobus to the many others whose efforts we have appreciated.

Each of us also has personal acknowledgments to make.

To Corinne, for all that you do.

—WALTER GERARD

Noted lepidopterist Dr. John C. Downey was my graduate advisor, but at that stage my interest in butterflies was limited to their being a large order in the class Insecta, and my collection reflected this. In 1975, Ray Sherwood, a senior biology major at Oral Roberts University, chose the butterflies of Tulsa County, Oklahoma, for his research project. I found that the butterflies of Oklahoma were not well known and there was no state checklist of butterflies available. I began by surveying the collections in the major state universities. At the University of

Oklahoma, W. J. Reinthal had made a small collection, mostly from Cleveland County. C. J. McCoy had done the same at Oklahoma State University, with many records for Payne County. Dan Shorter at Northwestern Oklahoma State University had many records for Woods County. Bill Carter at East Central State University had collected extensively in McCurtain County. There were also several other county records in all these university collections. For the past twenty-five years I have spent most of my spare time working on butterfly distribution in Oklahoma by accumulating hundreds of county records. Individuals who have contributed significantly with records include Ray Stanford, from Cimarron County; James Cokendopher, Comanche County; Chuck Harp, Oklahoma County; Don Arnold and James Fitter, Payne County; Bob Warren, Pittsburg County; Jeff Frey, Pete Loy, and Larry Robinson from Rogers and Tulsa counties; and Mike Tolliver from a number of counties. Others who have accompanied me on many collecting trips include my children—Penny, Lynelle, Nathan, and Lana—and Hal Reed and Chuck Conaway. Each of these people and all those who have contributed records in the annual Lepidopterists' Society Season Summary (published in *News of the Lepidopterists' Society*) have a part in this field guide. And most important, my wife Carol has been a source of encouragement and inspiration in all my activities for the past forty years.

—JOHN NELSON

To John Buettner and Vicki Stamback for your constant support, energy, humor, and encouragement and to the complex and beautiful world around us, which constantly inspires me.

—JOHN DOLE

BUTTERFLIES
OF KANSAS,
OKLAHOMA, AND
NORTH TEXAS

Introduction

Butterflies are probably the most recognizable group of animals in the world. They live everywhere that we live and attract our attention with their pleasing shapes, beautiful colors, and ability to fly. They are found in literature and works of art as symbols of freedom, life, and change. Author and lepidopterist Vladimir Nabokov often alludes to butterflies in *Speak Memory, Pnin, The Gift,* and *Pale Fire.* Butterflies are the central theme in such disparate works as Jo Brewer's *Wings in the Meadow,* a fictionalized account of a Monarch and her progeny; Miriam Rothchild's, *Butterfly Cooing Like a Dove,* a book about the influence of butterflies in art; and Robert Pyle's *Chasing Monarchs*, a travelogue following the fall migration of western Monarchs. Artist Vincent Van Gogh used butterflies as a symbol of hope in an otherwise bleak painting.

Butterflies are used in room decor; in craft items and various ornaments; on stamps, neckties, and clothing; as jewelry models in various cultures; in public exhibits; and in school science classes. While many people cannot distinguish a butterfly from a moth (see glossary), or readily identify any species other than the Monarch, almost everyone enjoys butterflies. Raising butterflies is becoming an increasingly popular endeavor, providing educational opportunities as well as pleasure (see chapter 1, Life Stages and Raising Butterflies). Homeowners are encouraged to make their yards friendly to butterflies and other beneficial invertebrates. Butterfly gardening is a popular pastime and, for some, even a business (see chapter 3, Butterfly Gardening). To naturalists and growing numbers of others, the excitement of a field of flowers hosting myriads of butterflies is a bountiful reward. This field guide to the common butterflies of Kansas, Oklahoma, and North Texas is intended to assist those interested in identifying, understanding, and enjoying butterflies.

The area covered encompasses most of the southern plains: Kansas, Oklahoma, and North Texas from Marshall to Dallas and west through Abilene and Midland to the New Mexico

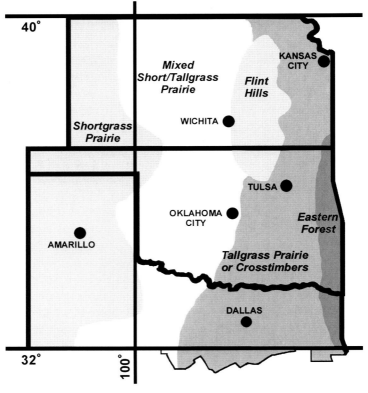

FIG. I.1. Ecoregions of the southern plains.

state line (fig I.1). The southern plains are divided by the 100th meridian, the traditional demarcation between the eastern United States and the more arid West. You can expect to find both eastern and western butterfly species in our region.

Typically the terrain is flat or gently rolling, broken by small mountains, canyons, arroyos, and streams. Characteristic plants are the grasses: remnants of tallgrass prairies in eastern Kansas and northeastern Oklahoma (fig. I.2); mixed-grass prairies in central Kansas, central and southwest Oklahoma, and the central part of North Texas; and shortgrass prairies in the high plains bordering the foothills of the Rocky Mountains in western Kansas, the Oklahoma Panhandle, and the Texas Panhandle (fig. I.3). Interspersed with the grasses throughout the plains are a wide diversity of flowering plants (forbs). Savanna woodland islands are also found throughout much of the region, and riparian woodlands occur along major streams. Along the eastern edge of southern Kansas, Oklahoma, and northern Texas, the prairie intergrades with the hardwood forest of the east. These features serve as corridors for movement from one area to another and allow a greater diversity of species in the plains by providing additional species of food plants. Soil types and depths vary widely in the region, which further influences the types of plants and their associated fauna.

Climatic characteristics of the plains are also quite diverse. Average annual rainfall ranges from 40 inches along the eastern edge of the region to only 10 inches along the western edge. Summer temperatures often exceed 100°F, while winter temperatures can drop to 0°F. To the consternation of butterfly watchers, wind is a frequent element of butterflying in the western parts of our area.

Many butterfly species are specialists, limited in distribution because their host food plant(s), sources of nectar, and

FIG. I.2. Tallgrass prairie of northeast Oklahoma in flower.

FIG. I.3. Shortgrass prairie of Cimarron County, Oklahoma.

habitat requirements are precisely defined. Examples are most hairstreaks, which generally feed on specific woody plants (trees or shrubs) and are found near the food source. Other species, called generalists, use a variety of host plants. The Gray Hairstreak (*Strymon melinus*), for example, has been reported to feed on more than 50 different kinds of plants and is found throughout the entire United States. Some species, such as the Eastern Tailed-Blue (*Everes comyntas*), are tolerant of extreme climatic changes and also inhabit the whole region. Others, like the Dainty Sulphur (*Nathalis iole*), Reakirt's Blue (*Hemiargus isola*), and Painted Lady (*Vanessa cardui*), are tropical and cannot survive the cold winters. Consequently, they move north each season from Mexico and South Texas all the way to Canada. Most of the butterflies illustrated in this guide are found throughout our region, and several have been recorded for every county in Kansas, Oklahoma, and/or North Texas. Other species have a more restricted range, as indicated by the distribution maps.

For those interested in comparing sizes of butterflies, the swallowtails have the largest representatives; the Eastern Tiger Swallowtail (*Papilio glaucus*) and Giant Swallowtail (*P. cresphontes*) have the greatest wingspans. Our smallest representatives are the Western Pygmy-Blue (*Brephidium exile*) and Southern Skipperling (*Copaeodes minimus*). Many of our species are sexually dimorphic; that is, males and females differ in color, pattern, or size. Others, such as the Question Mark (*Polygonia interrogationis*), Eastern Comma (*P. comma*), Southern Dogface (*Colias cesonia*), Sleepy Orange (*Eurema nicippe*), and Zebra Swallowtail (*Eurytides marcellus*), are polyphenic (having two or more seasonal forms, i.e. spring, summer, fall, or brood forms). The most beautiful butterfly is your choice—there is no such thing as an ugly butterfly! Oklahoma has its own official butterfly, the Black Swallowtail (*Papilio polyxenes*), while Texas chose the Monarch (*Danaus plexippus*) as its state insect.

Butterflies may be seen in any month of the year when the temperature rises above 60°F, even for only a day or two. Individuals of several species of the nymphalids and some pierids overwinter as adults and can be seen flying on warm winter days, especially in wooded areas. These hardy creatures include the Clouded Sulphur (*Colias philodice*), Orange Sulphur (*C. eurytheme*), Mourning Cloak (*Nymphalis antiopa*), Question Mark, Eastern Comma, and Goatweed Leafwing (*Anaea andria*). Butterflies are most numerous from May through September but are also rather common in our area from mid-March to mid-November. Some species appear only in the spring months of March through May, including the Olympia Marble (*Euchloe olympia*), Falcate Orangetip (*Anthocharis midea*), and Spring Azure (*Celastrina ladon*). Others, like the Ocola Skipper (*Panoquina ocola*) and Texan Crescent (*Phyciodes texana*), tend to be seen in late summer and fall.

In 1974, Field and colleagues reported that the butterfly fauna of only two other states—Delaware and Vermont—was less well known than that of Oklahoma. However, knowledge of Lepidoptera (butterflies and moths) in the southern plains has increased greatly during the past 25 years. Currently, the number of species recorded from Oklahoma is about 180, with a similar total for Kansas. Texas, because of its size and great ecological variety, has recorded 440 species, the most of any state. A complete list of the species known to occur in Kansas, Oklahoma, and North Texas is given in the appendix. The Internet has made information readily available to all interested individuals (see Organizations and Resources at the back of the book for contact detail). While we have broadened our understanding of the range and natural history of butterflies, much is still to be learned. New county and state records are discovered each year. Butterfly enthusiasts, with careful observation and record keeping, can contribute to gaining further information in the areas of butterfly life stages, host and nectar preferences, seasonality, mating behavior, life history, and conservation.

PART 1

Species
Accounts

*The 100 Regularly
Occurring Species*

Pipevine Swallowtail

Battus philenor

UPPERSIDE

UNDERSIDE

SIZE 2¾–5 inches

DESCRIPTION Upper surface of hindwing black with iridescent blue or blue-green. Underside of hindwing black with submarginal row of seven round orange spots in an iridescent blue field.

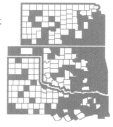

SIMILAR SPECIES Could be confused with other common predominantly black swallow-tails, including Spicebush, Black and black female Tigers. Note distinctive hindwing spots. Red-spotted Purple also has iridescent blue upperwings, but note its lack of tails and distinctly different underwing.

HABITAT A wide variety of open habitats, gardens, woods, and woodland edges.

MAJOR FOOD PLANTS Caterpillars feed on plants in the birthwort family (Aristolochiaceae) including Virginia snakeroot, netleaved snakeroot, and woolly pipevine (*Aristolochia serpentaria, A. reticulata, A. tomentosa*). Adults commonly nectar on a variety of flowers including thistles (*Cirsium*).

ABUNDANCE Common.

SEASON March to October.

COMMENTS This beautiful species can be attracted to the home garden by planting its host plant.

Zebra Swallowtail

Eurytides marcellus

UPPERSIDE SPRING FORM

UNDERSIDE SUMMER FORM

SIZE 2½–4 inches

DESCRIPTION Upper and lower surfaces of
wings have black stripes on a white to whitish
green background; hindwings have very long
tails. Early spring form is smaller, lighter colored and shorter tailed.

SIMILAR SPECIES The similarly striped
Eastern Tiger occurs in same area but has
yellow rather than white on wings.

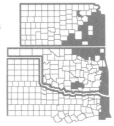

HABITAT Most common in moist woodlands
near swamps, streams, and other wetlands but commonly wanders
to dry woods, open fields, and brushy areas.

MAJOR FOOD PLANTS Caterpillars feed on pawpaw (*Asimina
triloba*) in the custard apple family (Annonaceae). Young plants are
preferred. Adults nectar.

ABUNDANCE Uncommon.

SEASON March to September.

COMMENTS Adults imbibe moisture from wet soil.

Black Swallowtail

Papilio polyxenes

UPPERSIDE, MALE

UPPERSIDE, FEMALE

UNDERSIDE

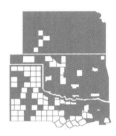

SIZE 3¼–4¼ inches

DESCRIPTION Upper surface of wings mostly black. Males have a yellow submarginal band and a marginal row of large yellow spots on both wings. Females have only a submarginal row of small yellow spots on both wings. Both sexes have an iridescent blue band (smaller on males than females) positioned between the yellow band and spot row. The underside is similar to the upperside except that the submarginal band or spots contain orange.

SIMILAR SPECIES Could be confused with other common predominantly black swallowtails including Spicebush, Pipevine, and black female Tigers; look for the orange-yellow spot row and submarginal underwing bands.

HABITAT A variety of open areas including fields, scrub, suburbs, marshes, and roadsides.

MAJOR FOOD PLANTS Caterpillars (see figs. 1.3 and 3.2) feed on plants in the parsley (Umbelliferae) and citrus (Rutaceae) families, including wild Queen Anne's lace (*Daucas carota*) and cultivated carrot (*D. carota*), parsley (*Petroselenium cripsum*), fennel (*Foeniculum vulgare*), and dill (*Anethum graveolens*). Plants in the citrus family (Rutaceae), such as rue (*Ruta graveolens*), are occasionally used. Adults nectar.

ABUNDANCE Common.

SEASON Late March to October.

COMMENTS One of the few butterflies with caterpillars that can become pests in the home garden (figs. 1.3, 3.2); clusters of caterpillars can denude parsley, dill, and fennel plants. The State Butterfly of Oklahoma. The Black Swallowtail is a Müllerian (inedible) mimic of the Pipevine Swallowtail.

Giant Swallowtail

Papilio cresphontes

UPPERSIDE

UNDERSIDE

SIZE 4–6¼ inches

DESCRIPTION Upperwings blackish with a bold yellow horizontal band across the forewing and a submarginal band across both wings. The underside is predominantly yellow with an irregular blue band across the hindwing.

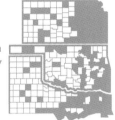

SIMILAR SPECIES From above, could be confused with the other common predominantly black swallowtails—note the horizontal yellow band across the forewing of the Giant Swallowtail. From below, yellow form Tiger and Zebra Swallowtails have stripes.

HABITAT Widespread, including streamsides, gullies, fields, open scrub, and suburbs.

MAJOR FOOD PLANTS Caterpillars feed on plants in the citrus family (Rutaceae), including prickly ash (*Zanthoxylum americanum*) and hop tree (*Ptelea trifoliata*). Adults nectar.

ABUNDANCE Common in low numbers.

SEASON Mid-April to August.

COMMENTS One of the largest butterfly species to occur in our area.

Eastern Tiger Swallowtail

Papilio glaucus

UPPERSIDE YELLOW FORM

UNDERSIDE YELLOW FORM

UPPERSIDE BLACK FORM

UNDERSIDE BLACK FORM

SIZE 3⅝–6¼ inches.

DESCRIPTION Large yellow butterfly with black stripes and margins and one tail. Female occurs in two forms: yellow (similar to male), and black (mimicking Pipevine Swallowtail). The black form shows faint stripe pattern. Forewing has one to two rows of submarginal yellow spots; underside of hindwing has one row.

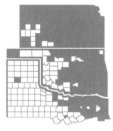

SIMILAR SPECIES Males and yellow form females may be confused with Two-tailed Swallowtails (not illustrated), which are restricted to far western counties, and Zebra Swallowtails, which are white to greenish white. Black form females are similar to Pipevine,

Spicebush, and Black Swallowtails, but note the faint stripe pattern showing through black on the Eastern Tiger.

HABITAT Openings and edges of deciduous broadleaf woods, including parks, gardens, and suburbs.

MAJOR FOOD PLANTS Caterpillars feed on many different species of trees and shrubs from a variety of families, including but not limited to ash (*Fraxinus*), cottonwood (*Populus*), wild cherry (*Prunus*), basswood (*Tilia*), birch (*Betula*), spicebush (*Lindera benzoin*), and lilac (*Syringa*). Adults nectar.

ABUNDANCE Common.

SEASON March to October.

COMMENTS One of our largest and best known butterflies. The black form female is a Batesian (edible) mimic of the Pipevine Swallowtail.

Spicebush Swallowtail
Papilio troilus

UPPERSIDE MALE   UNDERSIDE

SIZE 3–4 inches

DESCRIPTION Upper surface of wings mostly black with marginal band of whitish to blue spots and a submarginal bluish (female) or bluish green (male) patch. On inner edge of hindwing is a large orange spot. The underside of the hindwings has a marginal and a submarginal band of orange spots with blue in between. The underside of the forewing has a marginal and submarginal band of whitish spots.

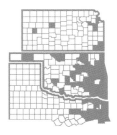

SIMILAR SPECIES Could be confused with other common predominantly black swallowtails; look for the hindwing marginal and submarginal bands of orange spots with the intervening blue replacing one of the submarginal spots.

HABITAT Open deciduous woods and nearby swamps, fields, roadsides, and parks.

MAJOR FOOD PLANTS Caterpillars feed on plants in the laurel family (Lauraceae), including spicebush (*Lindera benzoin*) and sassafras (*Sassafras albidum*), and in the magnolia family (Magnoliaceae), including tulip tree (*Liriodendron tulipifera*). Adults nectar.

ABUNDANCE Common.

SEASON April to October.

COMMENTS Spicebush Swallowtail is a mimic of Pipevine Swallowtail.

Checkered White

Pontia protodice

UPPERSIDE MALE

UNDERSIDE MALE

UPPERSIDE FEMALE

UNDERSIDE FEMALE

SIZE 1½–2½ inches.

DESCRIPTION White with a highly variable amount of gray to black checkered markings on the upperside of the wings. Female is typically more heavily patterned. Undersides range from pure white with only a few dark spots on the forewing (males) to faintly checkered with black and veins edged in yellow-tan.

SIMILAR SPECIES Could be confused with Cabbage Whites, which are almost entirely white with only one to two dark spots and black apex on the forewing. Olympia Marbles and female Falcate

Orangetips have the undersides of hindwings marbled with yellow, green, gray, or black.

HABITAT Occurs in a wide variety of open areas, including fields, pastures, roadsides, and dry weedy areas.

MAJOR FOOD PLANTS Caterpillars feed on plants in the mustard family (Cruciferae), including mustards (*Brassica*) and peppergrass (*Lepidium*), and in the caper family (Capparidaceae), including Rocky Mountain bee-plant (*Cleome serrulata*). Adults nectar.

ABUNDANCE Common.

SEASON April to November.

Cabbage White

Pieris rapae

UPPERSIDE MALE

UPPERSIDE FEMALE

UNDERSIDE

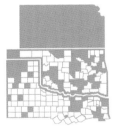

SIZE 1 ¾–2 ¼ inches.

DESCRIPTION Upperside of wings white with black or gray forewing tips and one (male) or two (female) submarginal forewing black spots. Underside of hindwing uniformly white with yellow-green cast.

SIMILAR SPECIES Similar to the Checkered White, Olympia Marble, and female Falcate Orangetip, but note distinctly different underwing patterns on those species.

HABITAT Found in almost any open space including fields, open scrub, gardens, roadsides, cities, and suburbs.

MAJOR FOOD PLANTS Caterpillars feed on many plants in the mustard family (Cruciferae) and a few in the caper (Capparidaceae) and the nasturtium (Tropaeolaceae) families. Adults nectar.

ABUNDANCE Common.

SEASON March to October.

COMMENTS This introduced species can be a pest on some garden vegetables, including cabbage and other related plants. Note that the cabbage looper (*Trichoplusia ni*), also a major pest, is the caterpillar of a moth, not of the Cabbage White. Cabbage looper caterpillars are glossy green and move in a characteristic humpbacked way. Cabbage White caterpillars are velvety green with a narrow orange stripe down the middle of the back and move smoothly across the leaf.

Olympia Marble

Euchloe olympia

UPPERSIDE

UNDERSIDE

SIZE 1⅜–2 inches.

DESCRIPTION Uppersides white with black to gray forewing apex and forewing bar. Hindwing underside has greenish gray marbling interspersed with white. Underside of forewing is mostly white with a limited amount of marbling. Both wing bases may have a soft rosy pink cast.

SIMILAR SPECIES Similar to the Cabbage White, Checkered White, and female Falcate Orangetip. Note distinctly different underwing pattern on Cabbage White and Checkered White and greater underwing marbling on Falcate Orangetip.

HABITAT Prairies, foothills, and open woodlands.

MAJOR FOOD PLANTS Caterpillars feed on members of the mustard family (Cruciferae), including cresses (*Arabis*), tansy mustard (*Descurainia*), and hedge mustard (*Sisymbrium*). Adults nectar.

ABUNDANCE Uncommon.

SEASON Mid-March to mid-May.

Falcate Orangetip

Anthocharis midea

UPPERSIDE MALE

UPPERSIDE FEMALE

UNDERSIDE FEMALE

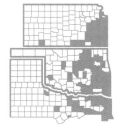

SIZE 1⅜–1¾ inches.

DESCRIPTION Male forewing upperside has a bright orange apex and is slightly hooked with a round black spot in center; hindwing upperside is unmarked white. Underside of hindwing has finely patterned gray-green marbling. Female is similar but lacks orange on forewing, has a blunter forewing apex, and is more heavily marbled below.

SIMILAR SPECIES Male is unique in our area but females could be confused with Olympia Marble, which has a bolder underwing pattern.

HABITAT Open, wet woods along streams, rivers, and swamps. Wanders occasionally to dry woods and ridge tops.

MAJOR FOOD PLANTS Caterpillars feed on a wide variety of plants in the mustard family (Cruciferae), including water cress (*Nasturtium*). Adults nectar.

ABUNDANCE Common.

SEASON Mid-March to mid-May.

COMMENTS One of the first butterflies in the spring and a welcome treat to find.

Clouded Sulphur
Colias philodice

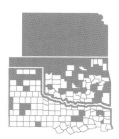

UNDERSIDE MALE

SIZE 1½–2¾ inches.

DESCRIPTION Upperside is bright yellow with black margins and a spot in the center of the forewing (black) and hindwing (orange). The underwings are pale yellow to greenish with a white-centered black spot in the center of the forewing and one to two silver, pink-rimmed spots in the center of the hindwing. Many individuals have a row of small submarginal black spots on the undersides. Female is either yellow or greenish white (white form) and has yellow spots in the upperwing black margin.

SIMILAR SPECIES Easily confused with the very similar Orange Sulphur, which usually has orange on the upperwings. However, some Orange Sulphurs have little orange; in such cases, look for the shadow of the upperwing black margin through the underside of the hindwing. The inner edge of the black margin will be between the margin and the underwing spot band in the Clouded Sulphur but will roughly parallel the submarginal row of black spots in the Orange Sulphur.

HABITAT Fields, lawns, alfalfa and clover fields, gardens, and road edges.

MAJOR FOOD PLANTS Caterpillars feed on many species in the pea family (Leguminosae), including a number of cultivated species such as alfalfa (*Medicago sativa*) and pea (*Pisum sativum*) and weedy species such as white clover (*Trifolium repens*). Adults nectar.

ABUNDANCE Uncommon to locally common.

SEASON Mid-March to November; most common in spring and fall.

COMMENTS You will rarely see the uppersides of this butterfly when it is at rest.

Orange Sulphur
Colias eurytheme

UNDERSIDE FEMALE ORANGE FORM   UNDERSIDE FEMALE WHITE FORM

SIZE 1⅜–2¾ inches.

DESCRIPTION Upperside is bright orange to yellowish orange with black margins and a spot in the center of the forewing (black) and hindwing (orange). The underwings are similar to those of the preceding species, Clouded Sulphur. Female is either yellow or greenish white (white form) and has yellow spots in the upperwing black margin.

SIMILAR SPECIES Easily confused with the very similar Clouded Sulphur, which is clear yellow on the upperwings. In the cases where some Orange Sulphurs have little orange, look for the shadow of the upperwing black margin through the underside of the hindwing. The inner edge of the black margin will roughly parallel the submarginal row of black spots in the Orange Sulphur but will be between the margin and the underwing spot band in the Clouded Sulphur.

HABITAT Fields, lawns, alfalfa and clover fields, gardens, and road edges.

MAJOR FOOD PLANTS Caterpillars feed on many species in the pea family (Leguminosae), including a number of cultivated species such as alfalfa (*Medicago sativa*) and pea (*Pisum sativum*) and weedy species such as white clover (*Trifolium repens*). Adults nectar.

ABUNDANCE Common to abundant. Much more common in most areas than the Clouded Sulphur.

SEASON March to November, but can also occur during the winter on warm days.

COMMENTS You will rarely see the uppersides of this butterfly when it is at rest. Some individual butterflies cannot be separated to species, and to make identification even more difficult, Orange and Clouded Sulphurs commonly hybridize. As a general rule, if the butterfly has any orange on the wing, it is considered an Orange Sulphur, and only the yellow butterflies are called Clouded Sulphurs.

Southern Dogface

Colias cesonia

UNDERSIDE
SUMMER FORM

UNDERSIDE
FALL FORM

SIZE 2⅛–3 inches.

DESCRIPTION Upperside forewings of both
sexes have a black margin and eyespot,
creating a yellow "dog's head" for which
this species is named. The forewing apex is
pointed. The hindwing upperside is mostly
yellow with some black marginal spots. The
underwings are pale yellow to greenish with
a white-centered black spot in the center of

the forewing and one to two silver, pink-rimmed spots in the center
of the hindwing. Females are similar, but markings are less bold.
The fall form has more pink on the undersides.

SIMILAR SPECIES Similar to Orange Sulphurs and Clouded
Sulphurs, but the Southern Dogface is larger with a pointed
forewing, and the dog's head often shows through on the underside. Could also be confused with the Cloudless Sulphur, which
lacks pointed forewing and dogface.

HABITAT Dry, open areas such as weedy fields, shortgrass prairies,
open scrub, open woodland, and road edges.

MAJOR FOOD PLANTS Caterpillars feed on several plants in the pea family (Leguminosae), including false indigo (*Amorpha fruticosa*), leadplant (*A. canescens*), black dalea (*Dalea frutescens*), purple prairie clover (*D. gattingeri*), alfalfa (*Medicago sativa*), and clover (*Trifolium*) species. Adults nectar.

ABUNDANCE Uncommon.

SEASON May to August.

COMMENTS You will rarely see the uppersides of this butterfly when it is at rest.

Cloudless Sulphur

Phoebis sennae

UNDERSIDE MALE   UNDERSIDE FEMALE

SIZE 2¼–3⅛ inches.

DESCRIPTION This large butterfly has yellow to whitish unmarked upperwings. The underside of the hindwing is pale yellow to greenish yellow with a variable amount of silver spots rimmed in pinkish orange and dark markings; males may be almost unmarked below while females are typically heavily marked.

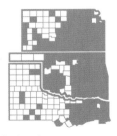

SIMILAR SPECIES Could be confused with Large Orange Sulphur, but that species is usually bright orange above and has a diagonal dark line on the forewing underside. Small Cloudless Sulphurs could be temporarily confused with Clouded Sulphurs, but the Clouded Sulphur has dark upperside margins.

HABITAT Gardens, parks, roadsides, fields, and open scrub, especially disturbed areas.

MAJOR FOOD PLANTS Caterpillars feed on plants in the pea family (Leguminosae), including wild senna (*Senna marilandica*) and partridge pea (*Chamaecrista fasciculata*). Adults nectar avidly.

ABUNDANCE Common.

SEASON April to November.

COMMENTS This large species migrates northward into our area from the south every year and often becomes common in gardens. The "cloudless" in the name refers to the unmarked upperwings.

Large Orange Sulphur

Phoebis agarithe

UNDERSIDE FEMALE

UNDERSIDE FEMALE WHITE FORM

SIZE 2¼–3⅜ inches.

DESCRIPTION This large butterfly has orange or whitish unmarked upperwings. The hindwing is pale orange or white (females only), with a variable amount of silver spots rimmed in pinkish orange and dark markings; males may be almost unmarked below while females are typically heavily marked. Forewing underside of both sexes has a dark straight submarginal line.

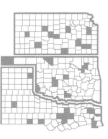

SIMILAR SPECIES Could be confused with Cloudless Sulphur, which is yellow above without a diagonal dark line on the forewing. Small individuals of the Large Orange Sulphur could be temporarily confused with Orange Sulphurs, which have dark upperside margins.

HABITAT Gardens, fields, roadsides, and open scrub.

MAJOR FOOD PLANTS South of our area, caterpillars feed on *Pithecellobium* and *Inga* species in the pea family (Leguminosae). Adults nectar.

ABUNDANCE Rare stray in the northern part of our area and uncommon in the southern part.

SEASON August to September.

COMMENTS Migrates into our region from the south each year.

Mexican Yellow

Eurema mexicana

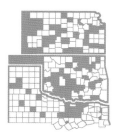

UNDERSIDE

SIZE 1¾–2½ inches.

DESCRIPTION Upperwing is creamy white to pale yellow with an indented black margin on the forewing creating a yellow "dog's head." Hindwing margin has some black and has projecting tail-like points. The underwings are creamy white to pale yellow with pinkish brown stippling.

SIMILAR SPECIES Separable from other sulphurs in our area by the pointed tails on the hindwing.

HABITAT Open, dry areas including weedy fields, prairies, open scrub, and gardens.

MAJOR FOOD PLANTS Caterpillars feed on members of the pea family (Leguminosae), including *Cassia* in our area and *Acacia* farther south. Adults nectar.

ABUNDANCE Uncommon.

SEASON May to September.

COMMENTS You will rarely see the uppersides of this butterfly when it is at rest.

Little Yellow

Eurema lisa

UNDERSIDE YELLOW FORM

UNDERSIDE WHITE FORM FEMALE

SIZE 1¼–1¾ inches.

DESCRIPTION Upperside of wings yellow or white (females only) with black margins, thickest along the apex. Underwings are yellow to white (female only) with small brown to black spots and smudges. Note two small basal dots.

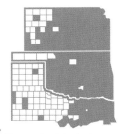

SIMILAR SPECIES Could be confused with Sleepy Orange, which is bright orange above, or with Mexican Yellow, which has pointed tails on the hindwing.

HABITAT Dry, open areas including roadsides, fields, open scrub, and gardens.

MAJOR FOOD PLANTS Caterpillars feed on plants in the pea family (Leguminosae), including partridge pea (*Chamaecrista fasciculata*), sensitive plant (*C. nicitans*), wild senna (*Senna marilandica*), and bundleflower (*Desmanthus*). Adults nectar.

ABUNDANCE Common.

SEASON April to November.

COMMENTS You will rarely see the uppersides of this butterfly when it is at rest.

Sleepy Orange

Eurema nicippe

UPPERSIDE

UNDERSIDE
SUMMER FORM

SIZE 1⅜–2¼ inches.

DESCRIPTION Upperside of wings medium to bright orange with black margins; black borders are not well-defined. Forewing has a small black cell spot. The undersides are brick red, brown, tan, or orange-yellow (summer), with a limited amount of small brown to black spots.

SIMILAR SPECIES Separable from other sulphurs by the orange upperwings and lack of large black or silver spots below.

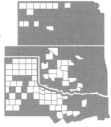

HABITAT Open woods, fields, scrub, gardens, vacant lots, road edges, and washes.

MAJOR FOOD PLANTS Caterpillars feed on plants in the pea family (Leguminosae), including partridge pea (*Chamaecrista fasciculata*), sensitive plant (*C. nicitans*), and wild senna (*Senna marilandica*), and on clover (*Trifolium*). Adults nectar.

ABUNDANCE Common to abundant.

SEASON June to October.

COMMENTS You will rarely see the uppersides of this butterfly when it is at rest.

Dainty Sulphur

Nathalis iole

UNDERSIDE SUMMER FORM

UNDERSIDE WINTER FORM

SIZE ¾–1¼ inches.

DESCRIPTION Tiny. Uppersides yellow to greenish yellow or white (rare) with black margins and other markings. Females are more extensively black than are males. Undersides are blackish green (winter form) to pale yellow (summer form); forewing has an orange or yellow patch at base of wing and black spots at outer wing edge.

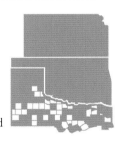

SIMILAR SPECIES The arrangement of black spots and orange patch on the underside of the forewing is distinctive.

HABITAT Open, dry places including weedy fields, grasslands, and road edges. Usually found in areas with open soil between plants or with low-growing or mowed plants.

MAJOR FOOD PLANTS Caterpillars feed on low-growing plants in the aster family (Compositae), including sneezeweed (*Helenium autumnale*), mayweed (*Dyssodia papposa*), greenthread (*Thelesperma megapotamicaum*), and on cultivated marigold (*Tagetes*) and cosmos (*Cosmos*). Adults nectar

ABUNDANCE Common to abundant.

SEASON April to November.

COMMENTS The smallest of the sulphurs in our area.

Harvester

Feniseca tarquinius

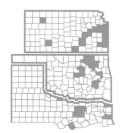

UNDERSIDE

SIZE 1⅛–1¼ inches.

DESCRIPTION Upperside of the wings is orange with black edges and black spots. Hindwing underside is orange to reddish brown with darker spots edged in white circles. The forewing underside has similar markings but shows more orange.

SIMILAR SPECIES Could be confused with any of the small brown hairstreaks, which tend to occupy the same habitats, but note distinctive underwing pattern.

HABITAT Deciduous or mixed woods along streams.

MAJOR FOOD PLANTS Caterpillars are carnivorous and feed on woolly aphids and sometimes scale insects or treehoppers; these insects suck sap from alders (*Alnus*), hawthorn (*Crataegus*), beech (*Fagus*), ash (*Fraxinus*), and witch hazel (*Hamamelis*). Adults feed on aphid honeydew and do not sip flower nectar.

ABUNDANCE Rare.

SEASON April to August.

COMMENTS This delicate beauty is the only carnivorous butterfly in our area.

Gray Copper
Lycaena dione

UPPERSIDE MALE   UNDERSIDE

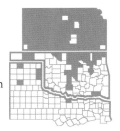

SIZE 1½–1¾ inches.

DESCRIPTION A large copper with the upperside dark gray, showing black spots on the forewing (more on the female), and the hindwing having a thin orange and black border on both sides. The underside is light gray with black spots.

SIMILAR SPECIES Similar to the Bronze Copper, which has orange forewing undersides.

HABITAT Moist fields and streamsides.

MAJOR FOOD PLANTS Caterpillars feed on plants in the buckwheat family (Polygonacea), including curly dock (*Rumex crispus*) and bitter dock (*R. obtusifolius*). Adults nectar avidly.

ABUNDANCE Rare.

SEASON June to July.

COMMENTS This beautiful species is widespread but local and always nice to find.

Bronze Copper
Lycaena hyllus

UPPERWING FEMALE

UNDERSIDE

SIZE 1¼–1⅞ inches.

DESCRIPTION The male has an upperside that is iridescent coppery brown on both wings, whereas the female is yellowish orange with bronzy purple marks on the forewing and bronzy purple on the hindwing. Both sexes have a broad submarginal orange band on both sides of the hindwings. On the underside both sexes are alike, the forewings being light

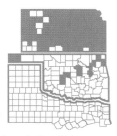

orange flecked with black spots and the hindwings being light gray flecked with black spots.

SIMILAR SPECIES Similar to the Gray Copper, which has a uniformly gray-white forewing underside. Female Bronze Coppers are distinctive above. The American Copper (not illustrated) is rare in far eastern Kansas but is smaller, with a narrower marginal orange band on the hindwing.

HABITAT Wet fields and marshes.

MAJOR FOOD PLANTS Caterpillars feed on plants in the buckwheat family (Polygonaceae), including curly dock (*Rumex crispus*), water dock (*R. verticillatus*), and bitter dock (*R. obtusifolius*). Adults nectar avidly.

ABUNDANCE Rare.

SEASON May to September.

COMMENTS The Bronze Copper is declining in much of its range.

Great Purple Hairstreak

Atlides halesus

UNDERSIDE

SIZE 1¼–1¾ inches.

DESCRIPTION Upperside is iridescent blue with black margins. The underside is dark gray with red spots basally and iridescent blue and green on the hindwing fringe above two tails. The abdomen is a striking orange below and blue above.

SIMILAR SPECIES Unmistakable in our area.

HABITAT Close to trees with mistletoe, and in open areas.

MAJOR FOOD PLANTS Caterpillars feed on plants in the mistletoe family (Loranthaceae), including mistletoe (*Phoradendron serotinum*). Adults nectar.

ABUNDANCE Rare to uncommon.

SEASON Early April to late September.

COMMENTS One of our most beautiful species. Females are larger than males.

Soapberry Hairstreak

Phaeostrymon alcestis

UNDERSIDE

SIZE 1¼ inches.

DESCRIPTION The upperside is brown and each hindwing has two
  tails. The underside is gray with a submarginal band of orange
  crescents on the hindwing and forewing followed by a white and
  black postmedian band on both wings. The key is to locate the
  white-centered black bars on both forewing and hindwing cells.

SIMILAR SPECIES The white and black bars in the center of the
  hind- and forewings distinguish the Soapberry Hairstreak from
  other hairstreaks.

HABITAT Hedgerows, woodland edges, and riparian areas near
  soapberry trees.

MAJOR FOOD PLANTS Caterpillars feed exclusively on soapberry
  (*Sapindus drumondii*) in the soapberry family (Sapindaceae).
  Adults nectar.

ABUNDANCE Common to abundant only where the food plant is
  abundant; rare otherwise.

SEASON May to July.

COMMENTS The caterpillar of this species is green with a double
  row of white lines along the back and a white line along each side.
  White hairs grow along the body.

Coral Hairstreak

Satyrium titus

 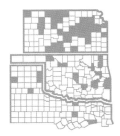

UNDERSIDE

SIZE 1–1½ inches.

DESCRIPTION The upperside is brown. The hindwing underside is gray-brown with a submarginal band of deep orange spots on the hindwing and scattered white-ringed black spots. Note the absence of a tail.

SIMILAR SPECIES The lack of a tail separates the Coral Hairstreak from other hairstreaks. The Coral Hairstreak could be confused with the Gray Copper or the Bronze Copper; however, they both have light gray undersides and black spots at the base of the hindwing underside. In addition, Coral Hairstreaks generally occupy drier habitats and are smaller than the coppers.

HABITAT Open areas, especially near woods or scrub.

MAJOR FOOD PLANTS Caterpillars feed on plants in the rose family (Rosaceae), including black cherry, wild plum, sandhill plum, and choke cherry (*Prunus serotina, P. americana, P. angustifolia, P. virginiana*). Adults nectar, especially on butterfly weed (*Asclepias tuberosa*).

ABUNDANCE Locally rare.

SEASON June to July.

COMMENTS Coral Hairstreaks rub their hindwings together like other hairstreaks, despite lacking a tail.

Banded Hairstreak
Satyrium calanus

UNDERSIDE

SIZE 1–1¼ inches.

DESCRIPTION Both wings are dark brown above and gray-brown below. The underside has the hindwing blue spot extending inward slightly beyond the adjacent orange spots and has a postmedian band of paired white dashes, of which the outer dashes are usually strongest.

SIMILAR SPECIES The Edwards' Hairstreak (not illustrated) has an underside postmedian band of brown spots circled by white on both wings. The Hickory Hairstreak (not illustrated) has a blue spot on the underside hindwing extending farther inward on the wing surface from the margin than in the Banded Hairstreak. In addition, the band of white dashes in the Hickory Hairstreak is wider, with the dashes more offset from one another, than in the Banded Hairstreak.

HABITAT Open areas next to or in woodlands.

MAJOR FOOD PLANTS Caterpillars feed on plants from a wide variety of families including hickory (*Carya*), oak (*Quercus*), walnut (*Juglans*), and ash (*Fraxinus*). Adults nectar.

ABUNDANCE Common.

SEASON May to June.

COMMENTS Males of the Banded Hairstreak can be found near hickory, oak, and walnut trees from dawn until 9:30 A.M., where they look for mates.

Henry's Elfin

Callophrys henrici

UNDERSIDE

SIZE 1–1⅛ inches.

DESCRIPTION The upperside of the wings is brown without a male stigma on the forewing. The hindwing underside is basally dark brown, with the outer part of both wings frosted. White dashes mark each end of the postmedian line on the hindwing. The hindwing has short tail-like projections.

SIMILAR SPECIES Males of the rare Frosted Elfin (not illustrated) have an upperside stigma on the forewing, and both sexes have a black spot on the underside hindwing near the tail-like projections. The Frosted Elfin has less contrast between the two sides of the postmedian line. Frosted Elfins may be endangered in our region.

HABITAT Woodland edges.

MAJOR FOOD PLANTS Caterpillars feed on a wide variety of plants from several families, including redbud (*Cercis canadensis*), which is a favorite host, plum (*Prunus*), blueberries (*Vaccinium*), holly (*Ilex*), and persimmon (*Diospyros*). Adults nectar.

ABUNDANCE Uncommon.

SEASON Late March to early May.

COMMENTS Individuals of this species rub their hindwings together like other hairstreaks. Look for the Henry's Elfin on or near its favored host, redbud, or on nearby soil, where it may be puddling.

Juniper Hairstreak

Callophrys gryneus

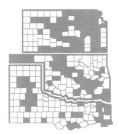

UNDERSIDE

SIZE 1–1¼ inches.

DESCRIPTION The upperside is orange with brown margins. The underside is pale green with white, brown, and black markings.

SIMILAR SPECIES No other green hairstreaks occur in our area.

HABITAT Old fields and scrub where junipers grow.

MAJOR FOOD PLANTS Caterpillars feed on trees in the cypress family (Cupressaceae), including red cedar (*Juniperus virginiana*) and other junipers. Adults nectar.

ABUNDANCE Locally common.

SEASON April to July.

COMMENTS The standard method of locating these hairstreaks is by "whomping" a red cedar tree and seeing what flies up. Caution should be observed, however, as caterpillars can be dislodged and they would have a difficult task finding their way back to the host. A better way to find the Juniper Hairstreak is to locate it while it is nectaring or imbibing salts from damp sand.

Gray Hairstreak
Strymon melinus

UPPERSIDE FEMALE

UNDERSIDE

SIZE 1–1 ¼ inches.

DESCRIPTION The upperside is dark gray on both wings with an orange spot by the tail on the hindwing. Both sexes have an orange collar and males have an orange abdomen. The underside is pale gray with a narrow submarginal stripe of orange, black, and white leading down to an orange eyespot on the hindwing.

SIMILAR SPECIES The gray underside combined with the lack of basal spots or dashes separates the Gray Hairstreak from other hairstreaks.

HABITAT Gardens, old fields, open woods, and prairies.

MAJOR FOOD PLANTS Caterpillars feed on a very wide variety of plants from more than twenty families but favor plants in the mallow (Malvaceae), pea (Leguminosae), and rose (Rosaceae) families. Adults nectar.

ABUNDANCE Common.

SEASON April to October.

COMMENTS One of the most common butterflies of our area. The butterfly constantly rubs its tails back and forth in typical hairstreak fashion.

Red-banded Hairstreak

Calycopis cecrops

 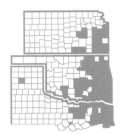

UNDERSIDE

SIZE ¾–1 inch.

DESCRIPTION The upperside is dark brown with iridescent blue. The underside is gray-brown with a conspicuous red-orange band that covers both wings submarginally.

SIMILAR SPECIES The bright red-orange submarginal band separates the Red-banded Hairstreak from other hairstreaks in our area.

HABITAT Woodland edges, brushy fields, and gardens.

MAJOR FOOD PLANTS Caterpillars generally feed on fallen leaves from plants in the cashew family (Anacardiaceae), including fragrant sumac (*Rhus aromatica*) and dwarf sumac (*R. copallina*), and in the bayberry family (Myricaceae), including wax myrtle (*Myrica cerifera*). Adults nectar.

ABUNDANCE Common.

SEASON April to October.

COMMENTS Oviposition takes place on dead leaves.

Western Pygmy-Blue
Brephidium exile

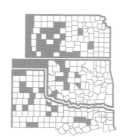

UNDERSIDE

SIZE ½–¾ inch.

DESCRIPTION The upperside wings of the Western Pygmy-Blue are blue basally (less so on females) and brownish orange out to the borders. The hindwing underside is white flecked with black basally, followed by brownish orange and then black and green eyespots on white submarginally. The fringes are mostly white.

SIMILAR SPECIES Its tiny size and brown underwings separate the Western Pygmy-Blue from other blues.

HABITAT Dry areas.

MAJOR FOOD PLANTS Caterpillars feed on plants in the goosefoot family (Chenopodiaceae), including lamb's-quarters (*Chenopodium*), saltbush (*Atriplex*), and tumbleweed (*Salsola iberica*), and in the carpetweed family (Aizoaceae), including horse purslane (*Trianthema*) and sea purslane (*Susuvium*). Adults nectar.

ABUNDANCE Common immigrant from South Texas.

SEASON June to July.

COMMENTS The smallest butterfly in North America.

Marine Blue

Leptotes marina

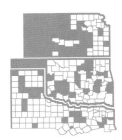

UNDERSIDE

SIZE ¾–1 inch.

DESCRIPTION Upperwings are brownish blue. The hindwing upperside has two small marginal black spots. The underside is graybrown striped with white and has two brown-ringed black spots on the hindwing margin.

SIMILAR SPECIES The zebra-stripe effect of white on the hindwing separates the Marine Blue from other blues in our area.

HABITAT Fields, weedy areas, and gardens, especially disturbed areas.

MAJOR FOOD PLANTS Caterpillars feed on the flowers and fruits of many species in the pea family (Leguminosae), including milkvetch (*Astragalus*), milkpea (*Galactia*), wild licorice (*Glycyrrhiza lepidota*), and alfalfa (*Medicago sativa*). Adults nectar.

ABUNDANCE Common.

SEASON June to September.

Reakirt's Blue

Hemiargus isola

UPPERSIDE MALE

UPPERSIDE FEMALE

UNDERSIDE

SIZE ¾–1 inch.

DESCRIPTION The upperside is blue (male) or blue basally and brown toward the margins (female). The hindwing upperside may have one or two submarginal black spots. The underside is pale gray with a submarginal row of prominent white-ringed black spots on the forewing and several white-ringed spots on the hindwing.

SIMILAR SPECIES Marine Blue and Spring and Summer Azures lack the row of large black spots on the forewing underside.

HABITAT Fields, open scrub, weedy areas, and prairies.

MAJOR FOOD PLANTS Caterpillars feed on the flowers, fruits, and young leaves of a wide variety of plants in the pea family (Leguminosae). Adults nectar.

ABUNDANCE Common.

SEASON April to October.

COMMENTS This species comes up from the south each year and repopulates the region. It cannot survive our winter. Larvae are attended by ants in a relationship known as myrmecophily (see glossary).

Eastern Tailed-Blue

Everes comyntas

UPPERSIDE MALE

UNDERSIDE

SIZE ¾–1 inch.

DESCRIPTION Tails are the key distinguishing feature for this blue. Males are blue on the upperside while females are dark gray. Females of the spring generation are gray with blue at the wing bases. The underside is pale gray to white with scattered black spots and markings. Orange spots are present near the tail on both upperside and underside.

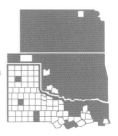

SIMILAR SPECIES This is the only tailed blue in our area.

HABITAT Fields, weedy areas, gardens, and suburbs, especially disturbed areas.

MAJOR FOOD PLANTS Caterpillars feed on the flowers, fruits, and young leaves of many species in the pea family (Leguminosae). Adults nectar.

ABUNDANCE Common.

SEASON March to November.

COMMENTS One of the most common butterflies in our region.

Spring Azure
Celastrina ladon

Summer Azure
Celastrina neglecta

UNDERSIDE SUMMER AZURE

UNDERSIDE
SPRING AZURE

SIZE ¾–1¼ inches.

DESCRIPTION On the upperside, the male is
light blue and the female is light blue with
black on the apex and outer margin on the
forewing. Look for the light blue while it is in
flight. The undersides of the Spring Azure are
light gray with a row of black crescents on
both wings. The hindwing has scattered black
marks. The Summer Azure is more whitish,
flecked with black on the underside.

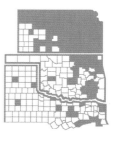

SIMILAR SPECIES Eastern Tailed-blue has tails. Marine Blue and
Reakirt's Blue have submarginal black spots on the hindwing
underside.

HABITAT Deciduous woodland openings and edges and scrub.

MAJOR FOOD PLANTS Caterpillars feed on many species from a wide range of families. Favorite hosts include wild plum (*Prunus americana*), dogwoods (*Cornus*), and New Jersey tea (*Ceanothus americanus*). Adults nectar, puddle, and visit dung.

ABUNDANCE Common.

SEASON April to May for the Spring Azure; late May to September for the Summer Azure.

COMMENTS The two species are nearly identical and best separated by time of year. Larvae are sometimes attended by ants (myrmecophily). They pupate in loose soil or under leaves.

Melissa Blue

Lycaeides melissa

UPPERSIDE FEMALE

UNDERSIDE

SIZE ⅞–1⅛ inches.

DESCRIPTION Uppersides are bright blue (males) or brownish blue with orange submarginal bands (females). Undersides are pale gray with white-edged black spots and a submarginal band of orange spots edged in iridescent blue. The hindwing margin is black with enlarged spots where the veins meet the margin.

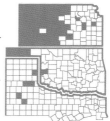

SIMILAR SPECIES The similar Acmon Blue (not illustrated) lacks enlarged spots where the veins meet the black hindwing margin. Female Acmon Blues have an orange submarginal band on the uppersides of the hindwing only. Other blues in our area lack the orange submarginal bands.

HABITAT Fields, prairies, roadsides, and open scrub, often in disturbed areas.

MAJOR FOOD PLANTS Caterpillars feed on a wide variety of plants in the pea family (Leguminosae), including milkvetch (*Astragalus*), wild licorice (*Glycyrrhiza lepidota*), sweetvetch (*Hedysarum alpestris*), deervetch (*Lotus purshianus*), and locoweed (*Oxytropis sericea*). Adults nectar.

ABUNDANCE Common.

SEASON June to August.

COMMENTS Larvae have honey glands and are attended by ants (myrmecophily).

Swamp Metalmark

Calephelis mutica

UPPERSIDE   UNDERSIDE

SIZE ⅞–1⅛ inches.

DESCRIPTION This small butterfly is dark brown to orange brown above with two submarginal bands of silver markings and scattered dark brown markings. The underside is bright yellowish orange, also with two submarginal bands of silver markings; the inner band is more square or abbreviated.

SIMILAR SPECIES The Northern Metalmark (not illustrated) is darker on the upperside, while the forewing silver band is more rectangular and connected on the underside. The Little Metalmark (not illustrated) is smaller and bright orange-brown above.

HABITAT Brushy woodlands near streams.

MAJOR FOOD PLANTS Caterpillars feed on swamp (*Cirsium muticum*) or tall thistles (*C. altissimum*) in the aster family (Compositae).

ABUNDANCE Locally rare.

SEASON May to mid-June.

COMMENTS The Swamp Metalmark is endangered or missing from much of its former range due to habitat loss. Wet meadows and marshes are disappearing at an alarming rate.

American Snout

Libytheana carinenta

UPPERSIDE

UNDERSIDE

SIZE 1½–1⅞ inches.

DESCRIPTION The greatly developed labial palps separate the American Snout from all other species. The forewings are squared off, their upperside orange and black with wide blackish borders and white subapical spots. The hindwings have one median orange area surrounded by gray-black. On the underside, the forewing is orange in the disc or central area and beyond, while the hindwing is gray to brown-black.

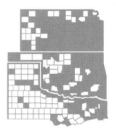

SIMILAR SPECIES When flying, the American Snout can appear to be one of many different species, but it is distinctive when you get a good view.

HABITAT Edges of deciduous woodland and open scrub containing hackberries.

MAJOR FOOD PLANTS Caterpillars feed on trees in the elm family (Ulmaceae), including hackberry, dwarf hackberry, sugarberry, and netleaf hackberry (*Celtis occidentalis, C. tenuifolia, C. laevigata, C. reticulata*).

ABUNDANCE Common.

SEASON Late May to September.

COMMENTS When resting, the American Snout looks like a dead leaf.

Gulf Fritillary

Agraulis vanillae

UPPERSIDE

UNDERSIDE

SIZE 2½–3 inches.

DESCRIPTION A large predominantly orange butterfly with black markings on both fore- and hindwing uppersides. It has white spots ringed in black in the forewing cell. The underside is brownish orange with large silvery white spots on both the forewing tips and the hindwing. The forewings are elongated.

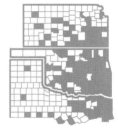

SIMILAR SPECIES No other large butterfly in our area has such predominantly orange upperwings and silvery white spots below.

HABITAT Open areas, scrub, fields, parks, and gardens.

MAJOR FOOD PLANTS Caterpillars feed on plants in the passion-flower family (Passifloraceae), including maypop (*Passiflora incarnata*) and yellow passionflower (*P. lutea*). Adults nectar.

ABUNDANCE Common.

SEASON Late May to October.

COMMENTS Another butterfly that migrates from the south to inhabit our area each summer. Note: It is not a true fritillary but a member of the Heliconiidae.

Variegated Fritillary

Euptoieta claudia

UPPERSIDE

UNDERSIDE

SIZE   1¾–2½ inches.

DESCRIPTION   On the upperside, wings are orange with black submarginal spots and are heavily marked with dark lines. The hindwing undersides are brown with pale cream on the median and marginal areas.

SIMILAR SPECIES   Other fritillaries have silvery white spots on the undersides. Crescents and checkerspots are much smaller.

HABITAT   Open areas, scrub, fields, parks, and gardens, often in disturbed areas with sparse vegetation.

MAJOR FOOD PLANTS   Caterpillars feed on a broad range of plants in several families, including violets (*Viola*), flaxes (*Linum*), spiderling (*Boerhavia erecta*), maypop (*Passiflora incarnata*), yellow passionflower (*Passiflora lutea*), moonseed (*Menispermum*), and plantain (*Plantago*). Adults nectar.

ABUNDANCE   Common.

SEASON   April to November.

COMMENTS   Males are much smaller than females. This species cannot withstand cold and must repopulate the area again in the spring from the south. See figure 2.2 for additional photo of Variegated Fritillary.

Diana Fritillary

Speyeria diana

UPPERSIDE MALE

UNDERSIDE FEMALE

UPPERSIDE FEMALE

UNDERSIDE MALE

SIZE 3¾–4¼ inches.

DESCRIPTION Unique. The male is black and orange on the upperside and brown and orange on the underside. The female is black and blue on the upperside, with the forewing underside also displaying black and blue. The hindwing underside is gray-black.

SIMILAR SPECIES The male Diana Fritillary may appear similar to other fritillaries;

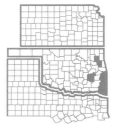

however, the Regal and Great Spangled Fritillaries have numerous silver spots on the hindwing underside.

HABITAT Openings in moist woodlands, especially near streams.

MAJOR FOOD PLANTS Caterpillars feed on plants in the violet family (Violacea), including downy blue violet (*Viola sororaria*). Adults nectar.

ABUNDANCE Rare.

SEASON Late June through August.

COMMENTS The female Diana Fritillary is thought to be a mimic of the Pipevine Swallowtail. Males emerge from the chrysalis first to establish territories before females emerge, ensuring an ample supply of males ready for mating.

Great Spangled Fritillary

Speyeria cybele

UPPERSIDE

UNDERSIDE

SIZE 3–3½ inches.

DESCRIPTION The upperside is brown basally, becoming orange and black at the outer margins. The hindwing underside has a wide buff submarginal band between silver spots. The forewing underside is brown with black marks.

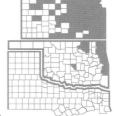

SIMILAR SPECIES When flying, the Great Spangled Fritillary appears similar to the male Diana Fritillary, but note the silvery white spots on the hindwings, which may not be noticeable until the Great Spangled Fritillary lands.

HABITAT Woodland edges and nearby moist fields.

MAJOR FOOD PLANTS Caterpillars feed on plants in the violet family (Violacea), including downy blue violet (*Viola sororaria*). Adults nectar.

ABUNDANCE Common.

SEASON May to September; most common May to June.

COMMENTS Females are larger than males.

Regal Fritillary
Speyeria idalia

UPPERSIDE   UNDERSIDE

SIZE 3–3¾ inches.

DESCRIPTION The forewing uppersides are rich orange with black markings and white marginal spots. The hindwing uppersides are black with white spots. Males have a row of orange submarginal spots, while on females this row of spots is white. The hindwing underside is dark brown with silvery white spots.

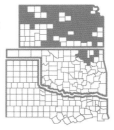

SIMILAR SPECIES The Great Spangled Fritillary has an orange hindwing upperside and a buffy submarginal band on the underside of the hindwing. The Variegated Fritillary has an orange hindwing upperside and no white spots on the underside of the hindwing.

HABITAT This species is associated with pristine tallgrass prairies.

MAJOR FOOD PLANTS Caterpillars feed on plants in the violet family (Violacea), including prairie violet, downy blue violet, lanceleaf violet, and birdfoot violet (*Viola pedatifida, V. sororaria, V. lanceolata, V. pedata*). Adults nectar.

ABUNDANCE Rare to locally common.

SEASON Mid-June to August.

COMMENTS The Regal Fritillary has virtually disappeared from the northeastern United States due to deterioration and destruction of its habitat.

Bordered Patch

Chlosyne lacinia

UPPERSIDE   UNDERSIDE

SIZE 1¼–2 inches.

DESCRIPTION The upperside of a typical Bordered Patch is black with a median orange-yellow band across both wings. The outer black band has two rows of white spots. The underside has a median yellow band bounded on each side by black, which is flecked with yellow spots and white marginal spots. However, this is an extremely variable butterfly.

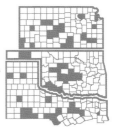

SIMILAR SPECIES Crescents and checkerspots are orange above and heavily lined with black.

HABITAT Open fields, weedy areas, gardens, and open scrub.

MAJOR FOOD PLANTS Caterpillars feed on a broad range of plants in the aster family (Compositae), including giant ragweed (*Ambrosia trifida*), annual sunflower (*Helianthus annuus*), and golden crownbeard (*Verbesina encelioides*). Adults nectar.

ABUNDANCE Common immigrant from South Texas.

SEASON June to August.

COMMENTS This butterfly has been described as the most variable in the nation.

Gorgone Checkerspot

Chlosyne gorgone

UPPERSIDE

UNDERSIDE

SIZE 1–1¾ inches.

DESCRIPTION Uppersides are orange, heavily marked with black lines and spots. The underside has brown and white zigzag marks and black submarginal spots. Pale arrowheads in the upperside border and in the underside margin and median areas distinguish this small species from other butterflies.

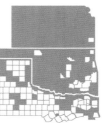

SIMILAR SPECIES The brown and white zigzag marks on the underside separate Gorgone Checkerspot from other crescents and checkerspots.

HABITAT Open fields, weedy areas, gardens, and woodland edges.

MAJOR FOOD PLANTS Caterpillars feed on plants in the aster family (Compositae), including sunflowers (*Helianthus*), giant ragweed (*Ambrosia trifida*), and marsh elder (*Iva xanthifolia*). Adults nectar.

ABUNDANCE Uncommon.

SEASON April to September.

COMMENTS Eggs are laid in large numbers on the host plant, and larvae feed together in early instars. Later they separate and feed alone.

Silvery Checkerspot

Chlosyne nycteis

UPPERSIDE

UNDERSIDE

SIZE 1½–2 inches.

DESCRIPTION Uppersides are orange, heavily marked with bold black lines, patches, and spots. The underside is white with brown lines and black spots. Some of the six submarginal spots on both upperside and underside have white centers. On the underside, the hindwing submarginal band is broken or disjointed.

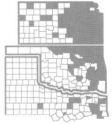

SIMILAR SPECIES The white-centered submarginal spots separate Silvery Checkerspot from other crescents and checkerspots.

HABITAT Fields and openings in woods, often adjacent to streams.

MAJOR FOOD PLANTS Caterpillars feed on plants in the aster family (Compositae), including black-eyed susan (*Rudbeckia laciniata*), prairie aster (*Aster umbellatus*), sunflowers (*Helianthus*), crownbeard (*Verbesina*), and goldenrod (*Solidago*). Adults nectar.

ABUNDANCE This species is uncommon to locally common.

SEASON May to September.

COMMENTS Females are larger than males.

Texan Crescent

Phyciodes texana

UPPERSIDE MALE

UPPERSIDE FEMALE

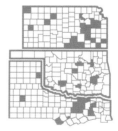

UNDERSIDE

SIZE 1–1½ inches.

DESCRIPTION The upperside of both wings is black with dark orange at the bases and white spots. The undersides are mottled white and brown; note the orange base to the forewing underside and the hindwing white median band. The forewing is strongly indented below the apex.

SIMILAR SPECIES The extensive amount of black on upperside and the indented forewing separate this species from other cresents and checkerspots. Some Bordered Patches also are predominantly black, but notice their median yellow band on the underside.

HABITAT Fields, weedy areas, gardens, and open scrub.

MAJOR FOOD PLANTS Caterpillars feed on plants in the acanthus family (Acanthaceae), including dicliptera (*Dicliptera bachiata*) and wild petunia (*Ruellia*). Adults nectar.

ABUNDANCE Common immigrant into our area from South Texas.

SEASON July to early September.

COMMENTS The Texan Crescent generally flies low to the ground.

Phaon Crescent

Phyciodes phaon

UPPERSIDE

UNDERSIDE

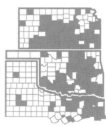

SIZE 1–1¼ inches.

DESCRIPTION This predominantly black and orange butterfly has a creamy white median band on the forewing upperside and underside. The underside has a forewing orange disc area and a hindwing marginal white crescent bordered in black. The rest of the underside is cream, intricately marked with brown lines.

SIMILAR SPECIES The creamy white forewing band and the hindwing marginal white crescent bordered in black separate the Phaon Cresent from other crescents and checkerspots.

HABITAT Low moist areas where the host plant occurs, especially near ponds and lakes.

MAJOR FOOD PLANTS Caterpillars feed on turkeytangle (*Phyla nodiflora*) and northern frogfruit (*P. lanceolata*) in the vervain family (Verbenaceae). Adults nectar.

ABUNDANCE Common to locally uncommon.

SEASON May to October.

COMMENTS The Pearl Crescent is seen in great numbers and may overshadow the Phaon Crescent, which is often overlooked because it flies low to the ground. The Phaon Crescent is worth the extra identification effort because of its attractiveness.

Pearl Crescent

Phyciodes tharos

UPPERSIDE

UNDERSIDE

UNDERSIDE
SUMMER FORM

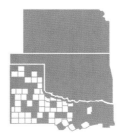

SIZE 1–1½ inches.

DESCRIPTION The upperside shows orange and black lines, circles, and crescents. The underside forewing is orange and black, while the hindwing is intricately marked with brown and varies from light orange (summer) to whitish and brown (spring). The hindwing underside has a white crescent partially or completely surrounded by brown.

SIMILAR SPECIES This common to abundant species overlaps the ranges of all other crescents and checkerspots and must be well studied to separate it from the others. Pearl Crescent lacks the pale bands of Phaon and Painted Crescents, the heavily marked forewing underside of Vesta Crescent (not illustrated), the intricate zigzags of the hindwing underside of Gorgone Checkerspot, and the white-centered hindwing spots of Silvery Checkerspot.

HABITAT　Fields, weedy areas, gardens, and open scrub, often in disturbed areas.

MAJOR FOOD PLANTS　Caterpillars feed on a number of perennial asters (*Aster*) in the aster family (Compositae). Adults nectar.

ABUNDANCE　Common.

SEASON　April to November.

COMMENTS　This is one of our most active and common butterflies. It is often found nectaring and puddling.

Painted Crescent

Phyciodes picta

UPPERSIDE

UNDERSIDE

SIZE 1–1½ inches.

DESCRIPTION The upperside is black and orange with a pale forewing median band and pale subapical spots. The hindwing underside is whitish to pale yellow with relatively few darker marks and lines. The forewing underside shows the pale median band.

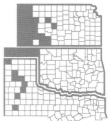

SIMILAR SPECIES The relatively unmarked hindwing underside and pale median band on the forewing separate the Painted Crescent from other crescents and checkerspots.

HABITAT Fields, weedy areas, and roadsides.

MAJOR FOOD PLANTS Caterpillars feed on field bindweed (*Convolvulus arvensis*) in the morning glory family (Convolvulaceae). Adults nectar.

ABUNDANCE Common.

SEASON May to September.

Baltimore Checkerspot

Euphydryas phaeton

UPPERSIDE

UNDERSIDE

SIZE 1¾–2¼ inches.

DESCRIPTION Upperside is black with white spots in the outer half and a band of orange crescents on the outer margin. The underside has orange spots basally followed by white spots and then an orange crescent marginal band, all separated by black. Note the orange palps.

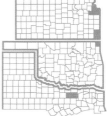

SIMILAR SPECIES No other species in our area has the distinctive black, white, and orange checkerboard pattern.

HABITAT Dry open forests, often with moist fields nearby.

MAJOR FOOD PLANTS Caterpillars feed on plants in a variety of families but prefer big-flower gerardia (*Aureolaria* [*Gerardia*] *grandiflora)* in the figwort family (Scrophulariaceae) and English plantain (*Plantago lanceolata*) in the plantain family Plantaginaceae). Adults nectar.

ABUNDANCE Rare.

SEASON May to June.

COMMENTS The eggs are laid communally and larvae feed from a silken nest. They diapause over winter, and when they emerge in the spring, they feed solitarily before pupating. The Baltimore Checkerspot is aposematically colored and is distasteful to birds.

Question Mark
Polygonia interrogationis

UPPERSIDE WINTER FORM

UNDERSIDE
WINTER FORM

UPPERSIDE SUMMER FORM

UNDERSIDE SUMMER FORM

SIZE 2¼–2½ inches.

DESCRIPTION The Question Mark has two
forms: in the winter form, the upperside
shows much orange on the forewing and hindwing, while the summer form shows much
orange on the forewing and black on the
hindwing. Both forms have several brown to
black spots on the upperside; note the horizontal black subapical mark between the

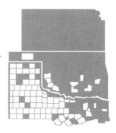

largest spot on the forewing and the margin. The underside is brown and leaflike with a white question mark shape on the hindwing. (Note that the dot in the question mark may sometimes be missing.) The summer form underside is mottled brown and black, while that of the winter form is more uniformly brown.

SIMILAR SPECIES The Eastern Comma is similar but without the upperside horizontal subapical mark on the forewing and with a comma shape on the hindwing underside.

HABITAT Woodland edges and openings and suburbs.

MAJOR FOOD PLANTS Caterpillars feed on plants in the elm family (Ulmaceae), including elms (*Ulmus*) and hackberries (*Celtis*), and in the nettle family (Urticaceae), including nettles (*Urtica* and *Boehmeria*). Adults rarely nectar on flowers.

ABUNDANCE Common.

SEASON March through November, but may occur on warm days during the winter.

COMMENTS This species is especially attracted to damp soil, animal scat, tree sap, and rotting fruit.

Eastern Comma

Polygonia comma

UPPERSIDE SUMMER FORM   UNDERSIDE SUMMER FORM

SIZE 1¾–2 inches.

DESCRIPTION The Eastern Comma has truncated forewing tips when compared to the very similar Question Mark. Like the Question Mark, it comes in winter and summer forms. In the winter form the upperside shows much orange on both fore- and hindwings; the summer form shows more black on the hindwing, and both forms have several brown to black spots on the uppersides. The leaflike underside is mottled brown and black—more uniformly brown in the winter form—with a white comma shape on the hindwing, the ends of the comma enlarged.

SIMILAR SPECIES Easily confused with the Question Mark, which is more common and sometimes has the dot missing from its underside question mark. The extra black subapical mark on the Question Mark's forewing upperside distinguishes the two.

HABITAT Woodland edges and openings and suburbs.

MAJOR FOOD PLANTS Caterpillars feed on plants in the elm family (Ulmaceae), including American elms (*Ulmus americana*), and in the nettle family (Urticaceae), including stinging nettle (*Urtica dioica*), wood nettle (*Laportea canadensis*), and false nettle (*Boehmeria cylindrica*). Adults rarely nectar on flowers.

ABUNDANCE Uncommon.

SEASON March to November.

COMMENTS The Eastern Comma is mainly found on rotting fruit and tree sap, but it does visit flowers occasionally.

Mourning Cloak
Nymphalis antiopa

UPPERSIDE

UNDERSIDE

SIZE 2¾–3½ inches.

DESCRIPTION Wing margins are irregularly shaped. The upperside is dark purplish brown with blue spots just inside a yellow border on both wings. The underside is dark brown streaked with blackish brown and with a cream border on both wings.

SIMILAR SPECIES This large butterfly with its distinctive pattern is not easily confused with other butterflies.

HABITAT Woodland edges.

MAJOR FOOD PLANTS Caterpillars feed on a wide variety of plants, mostly trees, in several families: willows (*Salix*), cottonwoods (*Populus*), birches (*Betula*), alders (*Alnus*), ironwood (*Ostrya virginiana*), maples (*Acer*), red mulberry (*Morus rubra*), elms (*Ulmus*), hackberries (*Celtis*), white ash (*Fraxinus americana*), dewberrys (*Rubus*), roses (*Rosa*), and American basswood (*Tilia americana*). Adults rarely nectar on flowers.

ABUNDANCE Uncommon.

SEASON April to September, but can occur any time of the year.

COMMENTS The Mourning Cloak is the longest living butterfly in the adult stage. This species visits flowers only occasionally but is especially attracted to tree sap and decaying fruit.

American Lady

Vanessa virginiensis

UPPERSIDE

UNDERSIDE

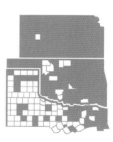

SIZE 1¾–2¼ inches.

DESCRIPTION The upperside is orange with brown margins and spots. The forewing has a postbasal black marking that is unconnected on the upperside. Many specimens have a small white dot in the outer orange. The underside is intricately marked with white lines and two large eyespots on the hindwing. The forewing is flushed with pink.

SIMILAR SPECIES The Painted Lady has postbasal black markings that are connected to each other on the forewing upperside and has four to five small eyespots on the underside of the hindwing.

HABITAT Open areas of almost any type.

MAJOR FOOD PLANTS Caterpillars feed on a wide range of plants from several families, especially everlastings (*Gnaphalium*) and pussytoes (*Antennaria*) in the aster family (Compositae). Adults nectar.

ABUNDANCE Common.

SEASON March to November.

COMMENTS The American Lady was at one time called Hunter's Butterfly, *Vanessa huntera*, which has since been reclassified to *V. virginiensis*.

Painted Lady

Vanessa cardui

UPPERSIDE

UNDERSIDE

SIZE 2–2½ inches.

DESCRIPTION The upperside is orange with brown margins and spots. The forewing has postbasal black markings that are connected to each other on the upperside. The underside is intricately marked with white lines and four to five small eyespots on the hindwing. The forewing is flushed with pink.

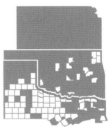

SIMILAR SPECIES The American Lady has postbasal black markings that are unconnected on the forewing upperside and has only two eyespots on the hindwing underside.

HABITAT Open areas of almost any type.

MAJOR FOOD PLANTS Caterpillars feed on a very broad range of plants in many families, especially thistles (*Cirsium*) in the aster (Compositae) family.

ABUNDANCE Common.

SEASON April to November.

COMMENTS The Painted Lady is unable to survive our winter. It migrates out of Mexico each year to repopulate its summer range.

Red Admiral
Vanessa atalanta

UPPERSIDE

UNDERSIDE

SIZE 2–2½ inches.

DESCRIPTION The upperside is brownish black with a median orange-red band on the forewing and a marginal orange band on the hindwing. White spots are visible both above and below on the forewing apex. The underside is mottled brown and black, with the forewing showing orange-red, blue, and white.

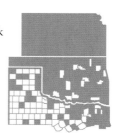

SIMILAR SPECIES The median orange band on the forewing and trailing orange band on the hindwing make this species difficult to mistake for any other.

HABITAT Open areas of almost any type.

MAJOR FOOD PLANTS Caterpillars feed on plants in the nettle family (Urticaceae), including stinging nettle (*Urtica dioica*), pellitory (*Parietaria pensylvanica*), false nettle (*Boehmeria cylindrica*), and wood nettle (*Laportea canadensis*).

ABUNDANCE Common.

SEASON April to November.

COMMENTS Males perch head downward, flying out to investigate an object that is passing by before returning to their perch.

Common Buckeye

Junonia coenia

UPPERSIDE

UNDERSIDE SUMMER FORM

SIZE 2–2½ inches.

DESCRIPTION The upperside is predominantly brown with a white band that partially encloses an eyespot and two orange marks in the cell on the forewing. The hindwing has a large and a small eyespot and an orange post-median band. The underside has reddish scaling in the hindwing winter form and light brown in the summer form. There is a dark brown submarginal stripe on the hindwing.

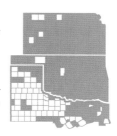

SIMILAR SPECIES The distinctive pattern separates this species from all others in our area.

HABITAT Fields, roadsides, gardens, and weedy areas; often found in dry areas with sparse vegetation.

MAJOR FOOD PLANTS Caterpillars feed on a broad range of plants from a number of families, including plantains (*Plantago*) in the plantain family (Plantaginaceae); butter-and-eggs (*Linaria vulgaris*) and gerardia (*Aureolaria* and *Agalinis*) in the figwort family (Scrophulariaceae); and turkeytangle (*Phyla nodiflora*) and northern frogfruit (*P. lanceolata*) in the vervain family (Verbenaceae).

ABUNDANCE Common.

SEASON April to November.

COMMENTS The Common Buckeye cannot withstand our winter and reinhabits our area in April.

Red-spotted Purple

Limenitis arthemis astyanax

UPPERSIDE

UNDERSIDE

SIZE 3–3¾ inches.

DESCRIPTION Black with iridescent blue. On the underside is a submarginal row of red-orange spots on both wings, with red-orange spots near the base. There is no tail.

SIMILAR SPECIES The Pipevine Swallowtail is similar but has tails and a submarginal row of large orange spots on the hindwing underside. Other dark swallowtails may appear similar

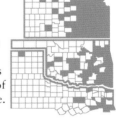

at first, but look for the tails and the white to yellow upperside spots.

HABITAT Forest edges and deciduous woods.

MAJOR FOOD PLANTS Caterpillars feed on a wide range of plants in several families: cherries (*Prunus*), willows (*Salix*), poplars (*Populus*), birches (*Betula*), alders (*Alnus*), hornbeams (*Carpinus*), apples (*Malus*), hawthorns (*Crataegus*), oaks (*Quercus*), and elm (*Ulmus*) are commonly used.

ABUNDANCE Common.

SEASON May to October.

COMMENTS A subspecies known as the White Admiral (*Limenitis arthemis arthemis*) occurs in the north. A wide zone of hybridization between the Red-spotted Purple and White Admiral occurs from the northeast to the northern plains.

Viceroy

Limenitis archippus

UPPERSIDE

UNDERSIDE

SIZE 2–3 inches.

DESCRIPTION Similar on the upperside and underside, the Viceroy is orange with white spots in the marginal black band and pronounced black veins. The hindwing is similar to the forewing but has a distinct black postmedian line.

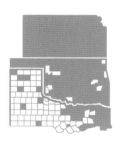

SIMILAR SPECIES The Monarch and the Queen do not have a black postmedian line on the hindwing.

HABITAT Woods and shrubbery along bodies of water and around wet areas.

MAJOR FOOD PLANTS Caterpillars feed on a wide range of plants in several families but prefer willows (*Salix*) and poplars (*Populus*) in the willow family (Salicaceae).

ABUNDANCE Common.

SEASON Late April to November.

COMMENTS Originally thought to be a Batesian mimic, the Viceroy is today considered a Müllerian mimic of the Monarch and the Queen.

Common Mestra

Mestra amymone

UPPERSIDE

UNDERSIDE

SIZE 1¾ inches.

DESCRIPTION White and gray on the uppersides with the outer portion of the hindwing pale orange. Undersides of the wings are orange with white bands.

SIMILAR SPECIES The distinctive white and orange pattern separates Common Mestra from other butterflies.

HABITAT Openings and edges of woodlands.

MAJOR FOOD PLANTS Caterpillars feed on plants in the euphorb family (Euphorbiaceae), including noseburn (*Tragia*).

ABUNDANCE Uncommon stray into the southern portion of our area; rare in the northern portion.

SEASON July to October.

COMMENTS Despite its slow flight, the Common Mestra is capable of straying into our area from its southern Texas breeding area.

Goatweed Leafwing

Anaea andria

UPPERSIDE MALE WINTER FORM

UNDERSIDE MALE WINTER FORM

SIZE 2½–3 inches.

DESCRIPTION The basic upperside color is red-orange with black markings, the female having more markings than the male. The underwings are gray and brown. The Goatweed Leafwing mimics leaves when it is perched vertically. This butterfly is both sexually and seasonally dimorphic, with the winter form having more markings and a more sickle-shaped forewing.

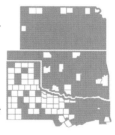

SIMILAR SPECIES The Tropical Leafwing (not illustrated) is a rare stray into our area and can be separated from the Goatweed Leafwing by the submarginal gray band it has on the hindwing underside.

HABITAT Inhabits a wide range of habitats, from open woodland edges to scrub areas.

MAJOR FOOD PLANTS Caterpillars feed on plants in the euphorb family (Euphorbiaceae), including goatweed (*Croton monanthogynus*), Texas croton (*C. texensis*), and woolly croton (*C. capitatus*).

ABUNDANCE Locally common.

SEASON April to October; overwinters as an adult and then flies April through May. May be seen in other months also.

COMMENTS The Goatweed Leafwing is attracted to tree sap and animal scat.

Hackberry Emperor

Asterocampa celtis

UPPERSIDE

UNDERSIDE

SIZE 2–2¾ inches.

DESCRIPTION The uppersides are brown, white, and black. The forewing upperside has one to two eyespots, with one dark bar and two dark spots in the cell. On the hindwing upperside is a submarginal row of large black spots. The underside is gray with eyespots on the forewing and hindwing and many dark lines. On the underside, the forewing cell

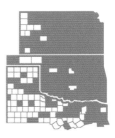

shows the same dark bar and two spots seen on the upperside.

SIMILAR SPECIES The Tawny Emperor does not have an eyespot in the forewing, is brighter buff above, and has two dark bars in the cell.

HABITAT Woodland edges, riparian areas, and yards where hackberry grows.

MAJOR FOOD PLANTS Caterpillars feed on several hackberry (*Celtis*) species in the elm family (Ulmaceae). Adults feed on sap and fruit and occasionally on carrion and dung. Adults rarely nectar.

ABUNDANCE Common.

SEASON May to October.

COMMENTS Often lands on humans to imbibe sweat. Males are smaller than females.

Tawny Emperor

Asterocampa clyton

UPPERSIDE

UNDERSIDE

SIZE 2–2¾ inches.

DESCRIPTION The uppersides are orange-brown and brownish black. On the forewing are two dashes in the cell, also visible from the underside. The hindwing upperside has a sub-marginal row of large black spots; the underside is gray brown with many dark lines.

SIMILAR SPECIES The Hackberry Emperor has an eyespot on the forewing and is grayer brown above.

HABITAT Woodland edges, riparian areas, and yards where hackberry grows.

MAJOR FOOD PLANTS Caterpillars feed on several hackberry (*Celtis*) species in the elm family (Ulmaceae). Adults feed on sap and fruit and occasionally on carrion and dung. Adults rarely nectar.

ABUNDANCE Uncommon.

SEASON June to October.

COMMENTS Males are smaller than females.

Northern Pearly-eye
Enodia anthedon

 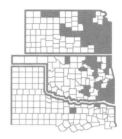

UNDERSIDE

SIZE 1¾–2¼ inches.

DESCRIPTION The brown upperside is rarely seen but has several large yellow-ringed submarginal black spots. The hindwing underside is brown with submarginal eyespots surrounded by a white line and darker brown lines. Note the black-based antennal clubs.

SIMILAR SPECIES The Southern Pearly-eye (not illustrated) is found in Oklahoma and Texas near cane (*Arundinaria*) but has completely yellow antennal clubs. The extremely rare Creole Pearly-eye (not illustrated), also found near cane, occurs in Oklahoma and as a stray in Kansas; each hindwing submarginal eyespot in this species is circled by white.

HABITAT Shaded woodlands near water.

MAJOR FOOD PLANTS Caterpillars feed on plants in the grass family (Graminae), including plumegrass (*Erianthus*), brachyelytrum (*Brachyelytrum erectum*), inland seaoats (*Chasmanthium latifolium*), reed canarygrass (*Phalaris arundinacea*), bottlebrush grass (*Hystrix patula*), and whitegrass (*Leersia virginica*). Adults do not take nectar but instead get nutrients from soil, scat, tree sap, and fruit.

ABUNDANCE Locally common.

SEASON May to September.

Gemmed Satyr

Cyllopsis gemma

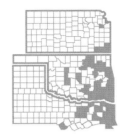

UNDERSIDE

SIZE 1⅜–1¼ inches.

DESCRIPTION Brown above and below with a silvery gray patch on the hindwing underside that contains four black spots.

SIMILAR SPECIES No other satyrs in our area have the silver patch with black spots.

HABITAT Grassy areas in open woodlands.

MAJOR FOOD PLANTS Caterpillars feed on plants in the grass family (Graminae). Adults do not take nectar but instead get nutrients from soil, tree sap, and fruit

ABUNDANCE Rare to uncommon.

SEASON April to September.

COMMENTS The silver spots on the hindwing underside give this species its common name.

Carolina Satyr

Hermeuptychia sosybius

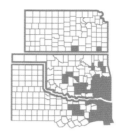

UNDERSIDE

SIZE 1⅛–1½ inches.

DESCRIPTION Uniformly brown uppersides without eyespots. The underside is brown with one prominent eyespot on the forewing and three on the hindwing. There are several less prominent eyespots as well. The eyespots have light centers. The undersides also have dark vertical lines.

SIMILAR SPECIES The Little Wood-Satyr has two prominent eyespots on the forewing and two on the hindwing, appearing on the upperside as well as the underside.

HABITAT Woodlands and grassy openings.

MAJOR FOOD PLANTS Caterpillars feed on plants in the grass family (Graminae), including orchard grass (*Dactylis glomerata*). Adults do not take nectar but instead get nutrients from soil, tree sap, and fruit.

ABUNDANCE Locally common.

SEASON June to September.

COMMENTS Flies slowly and close to the ground.

Little Wood-Satyr

Megisto cymela

UPPERSIDE

UNDERSIDE

SIZE 1¾ inches.

DESCRIPTION Brown with two black, yellow-ringed eyespots on both upperside and underside of each wing. The undersides have dark brown vertical lines.

SIMILAR SPECIES The Carolina Satyr has only one prominent eyespot on the forewing and the uppersides have no eyespots.

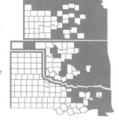

HABITAT Deciduous woods and grassy openings.

MAJOR FOOD PLANTS Caterpillars feed on plants in the grass family (Graminae), including orchard grass (*Dactylis glomerata*). Adults only occasionally take nectar, mainly feeding on tree sap and aphid honeydew.

ABUNDANCE Locally common.

SEASON May to August.

COMMENTS Flies low among the vegetation.

Common Wood-Nymph

Cercyonis pegala

UNDERSIDE DARK FORM

UNDERSIDE
YELLOW FORM

SIZE 2–3 inches.

DESCRIPTION A dark brown butterfly with two large eyespots, which may be surrounded with a large yellow patch on the forewing upperside and underside. The yellow is absent on western forms in our area. The hindwing has several smaller eyespots visible on both surfaces and is heavily striated with dark lines below.

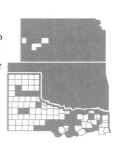

SIMILAR SPECIES Other satyrs in our area are smaller and lack the large yellow patch.

HABITAT Prairies, open meadows, and woodlands.

MAJOR FOOD PLANTS Caterpillars feed on plants in the grass family (Graminae), including bluestems (*Andropogon*) and purpletop (*Tridens flavus*). Adults nectar and occasionally feed on sap and scat.

ABUNDANCE Common.

SEASON May to October.

COMMENTS The Common Wood-Nymph has one brood a year, with females being larger than males. In northern and western populations, the yellow patch may be missing, replaced with solid brown around the eyespots.

Monarch

Danaus plexippus

UPPERSIDE MALE

UPPERSIDE FEMALE

UNDERSIDE

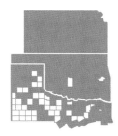

SIZE 3½–4 inches.

DESCRIPTION Orange above with submarginal and marginal black with white spots on the forewing and marginal black with white spots on the hindwing. Undersides are a dull orange. The veins are outlined in black. Males have a black scent patch on the hindwings.

SIMILAR SPECIES The Viceroy has a black postmedian line on the hindwing. The Queen has a submarginal row of white spots on the forewing.

HABITAT Fields, roadsides, weedy areas, and parks.

MAJOR FOOD PLANTS Caterpillars feed on numerous milkweeds (*Asclepias*) in the milkweed family (Asclepiadaceae). Adults nectar.

ABUNDANCE Common.

SEASON April to October.

COMMENTS The spring migration northward is virtually unnoticed. The fall migration can be spectacular with Monarchs coming through our area in great numbers.

Queen

Danaus gilippus

UPPERSIDE

UNDERSIDE

SIZE 3–3½ inches.

DESCRIPTION A brown-orange butterfly with upperside black margins, a white submarginal row of spots on the forewing, and white edgings on the black veins of the hindwing. The underside is similar to the upperside.

SIMILAR SPECIES The Viceroy is brighter orange with a thin black submarginal line on the hindwing. The Monarch is brighter orange above with black veins.

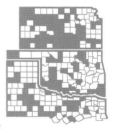

HABITAT Fields, roadsides, weedy areas, and parks.

MAJOR FOOD PLANTS Caterpillars feed on numerous milkweeds (*Asclepias*) in the milkweed family (Asclepiadaceae).

ABUNDANCE Common in the southern portion of our area; regularly strays northward.

SEASON July to September.

COMMENTS The Queen cannot survive our winter but it could occur anywhere in our area during the summer and fall.

Silver-spotted Skipper

Epargyreus clarus

UPPERSIDE

UNDERSIDE

SIZE 1¾–2⅝ inches.

DESCRIPTION Wings are dark brown. Upperside forewing has transparent pale to translucent spots. The hindwing is lobed with a bright white band in the center.

SIMILAR SPECIES Hoary Edge is also large, but white is along the outer margin of the hindwing, not in the center.

HABITAT Widespread in fields, scrub, open woods, and suburbs.

MAJOR FOOD PLANTS Caterpillars feed on plants in the legume family (Leguminosae) family, especially woody legumes such as black locust (*Robinia pseudoacacia*), honey locust (*Gleditsia triacanthos*), and false indigo (*Amorpha*). Adults nectar.

ABUNDANCE Common.

SEASON April to October.

COMMENTS One of our largest regular skippers--easy to watch and identify.

Hoary Edge
Achalarus lyciades

UPPERSIDE

UNDERSIDE

SIZE ¾–1¹⁵⁄₁₆ inches.

DESCRIPTION Upperside of wings is dark brown; the forewing has a band of irregular gold-brown spots. The undersides have a mottled pattern of black and brown with a distinctive wide silvery white band along most of the outer hindwing margin.

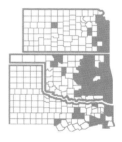

SIMILAR SPECIES The Silver-spotted Skipper is also large and brown but has a white band in the center of the hindwing underside.

HABITAT Sunny areas in open woods and brush.

MAJOR FOOD PLANTS Caterpillars feed on plants in the legume family (Leguminosae), including tickclover (*Desmodium*) and occasionally wild indigo (*Baptisia*) and bush clover (*Lespedeza*). Adults nectar.

ABUNDANCE Uncommon.

SEASON May to October.

Southern Cloudywing

Thorybes bathyllus

UPPERSIDE

UNDERSIDE

SIZE 1⁵⁄₁₆–1⁷⁄₈ inches.

DESCRIPTION Upperside dark brown with numerous rectangular whitish spots in two bands on the forewing. Spots can vary from large to small. Antennae have a white patch just where the club bends. Hindwing fringe may be light colored to white. Undersides are mottled brown and black with forewing spots showing through.

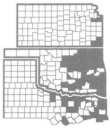

SIMILAR SPECIES Easily confused with Northern Cloudywing and Confused Cloudywing (not illustrated). Spots on Southern Cloudywings are usually larger than on Northern Cloudywings, but spring brood individuals may have small spots; note the white patch on antennae of Southern Cloudywings.

HABITAT Dry weedy areas, fields, prairies, and roadsides.

MAJOR FOOD PLANTS Caterpillars feed on plants in the pea family (Leguminosae), including butterfly pea (*Centrosema virginianum*), tickclovers (*Desmodium*), bush clovers (*Lespedeza*), wild bean (*Strophostyles*), and red clover (*Trifolium pratense*). Adults nectar.

ABUNDANCE Common but rarely numerous in any one location.

SEASON April to October.

COMMENTS The cloudywings can be difficult species to tell apart. View additional pictures and read other references (see Preface for suggested references).

Northern Cloudywing

Thorybes pylades

UPPERSIDE

UNDERSIDE

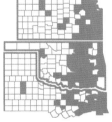

SIZE 1¼–1⅞ inches.

DESCRIPTION Upperside dark brown with numerous spots in two bands on the forewing. Spots are small. Undersides are mottled brown and black with forewing spots showing through.

SIMILAR SPECIES Easily confused with Southern Cloudywing and Confused Cloudywing (not illustrated). Spots on Southern Cloudywings are usually larger than on Northern Cloudywings but spring brood Southern Cloudywings may have small spots; note the white patch on antennae and the white or gray "face" of Southern Cloudywings.

HABITAT Open scrub or woodlands.

MAJOR FOOD PLANTS Caterpillars feed on various plants in the pea family (Leguminosae), including Nuttall milkvetch (*Astragalus nuttallianus*), tickclovers (*Desmodium*), bush clovers (*Lespedeza*), alfalfa (*Medicago sativa*), clovers (*Trifolium*), and American vetch (*Vicia americana*). Adults nectar.

ABUNDANCE Common but rarely numerous in any one location.

SEASON April to September.

COMMENTS See comments under Southern Cloudywing.

Hayhurst's Scallopwing

Staphylus hayhurstii

UPPERSIDE MALE

UPPERSIDE FEMALE

SIZE 1–1¼ inches.

DESCRIPTION Upperside is dark brown with two darker bands across each wing; forewing has a few tiny translucent dots. Males are darker than females. Hindwing margins are scalloped; fringe on both wings is checkered black and tan.

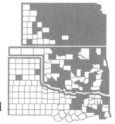

SIMILAR SPECIES The scalloped hindwing and dark color separate this species from others.

HABITAT Open woods and scrub, roadsides, and gardens.

MAJOR FOOD PLANTS Caterpillars feed on lamb's-quarters (*Chenopodium album*) in the goosefoot family (Chenopodiaceae). Adults nectar.

ABUNDANCE Uncommon to common but rarely numerous in any one location.

SEASON May to September.

Horace's Duskywing

Erynnis horatius

UPPERSIDE MALE

UPPERSIDE FEMALE

UNDERSIDE

SIZE 1 ⁷⁄₁₆–1 ¹⁵⁄₁₆ inches.

DESCRIPTION Upperside of forewing in males is dark brown with little pattern evident. Upperside of female's forewing is dark brown with a contrasting pattern and several large transparent spots. Fringes are brown. Underside of hindwing is mottled brown with marginal rows of pale spots.

SIMILAR SPECIES The duskywings are one of the most difficult groups of butterflies to distinguish. Horace's is probably the most common in our area and is easily confused with Wild Indigo

Duskywing, which tends to be darker, and Juvenal's Duskywing (not illustrated), which has two pale subapical spots on the hindwing underside. Juvenal's Duskywing flies only from March to May.

HABITAT Open woodlands and scrub, fields, roadsides, and gardens.

MAJOR FOOD PLANTS Caterpillars feed on numerous oaks (*Quercus*) in the beech family (Fagaceae). Adults nectar.

ABUNDANCE Common but rarely numerous.

SEASON April to October.

COMMENTS Duskywings are another difficult group of species. Check out other references for tips on telling them apart (see Preface for suggested references).

Funereal Duskywing
Erynnis funeralis

UPPERSIDE

UNDERSIDE

SIZE 1⁵⁄₁₆–1¾ inches.

DESCRIPTION Upperside of forewing is dark brown to blackish with a contrasting pattern and several transparent spots. Hindwing fringe is white. Underside of hindwing is mottled brown with marginal rows of pale spots.

SIMILAR SPECIES The Funereal Duskywing is the only regularly occurring duskywing in our area with white hindwing fringes. Also, the

forewing is narrower and more pointed than in other duskywings in our area.

HABITAT Warm or arid lowlands, roadsides.

MAJOR FOOD PLANTS Caterpillars feed on plants in the pea family (Leguminosae), including sesbania (*Sesbania macrocarpa*), western indigo (*Indigofera miniata*), and alfalfa (*Medicago sativa*). Adults nectar.

ABUNDANCE Common.

SEASON May to August.

COMMENTS See comments under Horace's Duskywing.

Wild Indigo Duskywing

Erynnis baptisiae

UPPERSIDE MALE

UNDERSIDE

SIZE 1⅜–1⅝ inches.

DESCRIPTION Upperside of forewing is dark brown to blackish with a contrasting pattern and several transparent spots. Basal one-third of forewing often appears darker than the rest of the wing. Fringes are brown. Females are more mottled and contrasting than males. Underside of hindwing is mottled brown with marginal rows of pale spots.

SIMILAR SPECIES The Wild Indigo Duskywing is easily confused with Horace's Duskywing, which tends to be paler.

HABITAT Open woods and scrub, roadsides, and fields.

MAJOR FOOD PLANTS Caterpillars feed on plants in the pea (Leguminosae) family, including wild blue indigo, plains wild indigo, and white wild indigo (*Baptisia australis*, *B. bracteata*, *B. lactea*), rattlebox (*Crotalaria sagittalis*), and crown vetch (*Coronilla varia*). Adults nectar.

ABUNDANCE Common.

SEASON April to September.

COMMENTS See comments under Horace's Duskywing.

Common Checkered-Skipper

Pyrgus communis

UPPERSIDE MALE

UPPERSIDE FEMALE

UNDERSIDE

SIZE 1–1½ inches.

DESCRIPTION Upperside has small to large white spots on black, forming bands across both wings. Body and wing bases are often overlaid with blue-gray hairs. Fringes are checkered. Males are whiter than females. Underside is mottled white with dark gray or olive bands and splotches.

SIMILAR SPECIES Distinctive in our area, but other checkered-skippers occur to the south and west.

HABITAT Open, sunny places with low vegetation and some bare soil, including weedy areas, prairies, fields, roadsides, gardens, and openings in woods and scrub.

MAJOR FOOD PLANTS Caterpillars feed on many plants in the mallow family (Malvaceae), including hollyhock (*Althaea*), poppy mallow (*Callirhoë*), modiola (*Modiola caroliniana*), common mallow (*Malva*), sida (*Sida*), and globe mallows (*Sphaeralcea*). Adults nectar.

ABUNDANCE Common.

SEASON Late March to early November.

COMMENTS Adults are low flying.

Common Sootywing

Pholisora catullus

UPPERSIDE MALE

UPPERSIDE FEMALE

SIZE 1–1⁵⁄₁₆ inches.

DESCRIPTION Upperside is glossy black to dark brown with small white spots on outer third of the forewing and on the head. Female has more white spots on the forewing than the male and a has submarginal row of spots on the hindwing. Underside is similar to upperside.

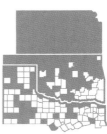

SIMILAR SPECIES Separable from Hayhurst's Scallopwing by lack of scalloped hindwing and from duskywings by uniformly dark coloration.

HABITAT Open or disturbed areas such as weedy fields, gardens, roadsides, and fields.

MAJOR FOOD PLANTS Caterpillars feed on plants in the amaranth family (Amaranthaceae), including amaranths (*Amaranthus*) and cultivated cockscomb (*Celosia argentea*), and in the goosefoot family (Chenophodiacea), including lamb's-quarters (*Chenopodium*).

ABUNDANCE Common but rarely numerous.

SEASON April to September.

Clouded Skipper

Lerema accius

UPPERSIDE MALE

UPPERSIDE FEMALE

UNDERSIDE

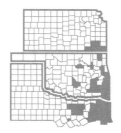

SIZE 1¼–1¾ inches.

DESCRIPTION Both sides of wings are dark brown. Forewing has three subapical white spots; spots are large on females and small on males. Females have additional forewing spots. Underside of hindwing has dark and light patches and a distinctive violet sheen when fresh.

SIMILAR SPECIES Fresh Clouded Skippers with violet sheen are beautiful and distinctive. Worn individuals can be confused with Dun Skippers, which are lighter brown with a hindwing underside either unmarked or showing a faint submarginal spot band. Female

Zabulon and Hobomok (not illustrated) Skippers have larger white forewing spots than Clouded Skippers.

HABITAT Moist grassy areas in or often some distance from woods.

MAJOR FOOD PLANTS Caterpillars feed on various plants in the grass family (Graminae), including bluestem (*Andropogon*), silver plumegrass (*Erianthus alopecuroides*), witchgrass (*Panicum capillare*), Johnson grass (*Sorghum halapense*), St. Augustine grass (*Stenotaphrum secundatum*), and corn (*Zea mays*). Adults nectar.

ABUNDANCE Common.

SEASON May to September.

Least Skipper

Ancyloxypha numitor

UPPERSIDE

UNDERSIDE

SIZE ⅞–1⅛ inches.

DESCRIPTION Forewing upperside is brown and hindwing is orange with a wide black border. Underside of forewing is black with an orange margin at the tip and leading edge; hindwing is orange. Black of forewing underside is often not visible when butterfly is at rest. This species is tiny.

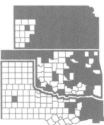

SIMILAR SPECIES The mostly dark upperside, small size, and moist habitat separate this species from Orange and Southern Skipperlings (not illustrated).

HABITAT Moist open places with tall grasses, such as marshes and ditches, and edges of streams, ponds, and lakes.

MAJOR FOOD PLANTS Caterpillars feed on various plants in the grass family (Graminae), including southern wild rice (*Zizaniopsis miliacea*), cultivated rice (*Oryza sativa*), rice cutgrass (*Leersia oryzoides*), bluegrass (*Poa*), cordgrass (*Spartina*), foxtail (*Setaria*), and panic grass (*Panicum*).

ABUNDANCE Common in limited areas.

SEASON April to October.

COMMENTS One of our smallest butterflies.

Fiery Skipper

Hylephila phyleus

UPPERSIDE MALE

UNDERSIDE MALE

UPPERSIDE FEMALE

UNDERSIDE FEMALE

SIZE 1¼–1½ inches.

DESCRIPTION Males are yellow-orange above with toothed black margins and a wide black stigma on the forewing. Underside of the hindwing is yellow-orange with scattered small black to brown spots. Some males have few spots. Females are dark brown above, irregularly marked with orange spots and splotches. Underside of hindwing is dull yellowish brown to orange with pale spots tipped in dark brown. Underwing spots tend to be smaller and more sharply defined on males than females. Antennae of both sexes are shorter than in other similar skippers.

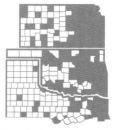

SIMILAR SPECIES Spots on the hindwing and short antennae separate Fiery Skippers from similar skippers. Worn Fiery Skippers may
have few spots, making them difficult to identify.

HABITAT Sunny, open areas such as fields, lawns, gardens, roadsides, and scrub.

MAJOR FOOD PLANTS Caterpillars feed on plants in the grass
family (Graminae), including Bermuda grass (*Cynodon dactylon*),
bentgrass (*Agrostis*), lovegrass (*Eragrostis hypnoides*), bluegrass
(*Poa pratensis*), and St. Augustine grass (*Stenotaphrum
secundatum*).

ABUNDANCE Common to abundant.

SEASON April to November.

Green Skipper

Hesperia viridis

UPPERSIDE MALE

UNDERSIDE

SIZE 1–1½ inches.

DESCRIPTION Uppersides are bright orange with wide brown margins and several pale spots in the margin. Males have a long thin black stigma, and females have more pale spots than males. Hindwing is olive to yellow-orange with distinct large white spots.

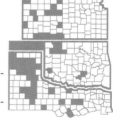

SIMILAR SPECIES The large white spots distinguish this species in our area. The Dotted Skipper has much smaller spots on the hindwing.

HABITAT Grassy areas in scrub, prairies, ravines, and roadsides.

MAJOR FOOD PLANTS Caterpillars feed on various plants in the grass family (Graminae), including blue grama (*Bouteloua gracilis*), sideoats grama (*Bouteloua curtipendula*), buffalograss (*Buchloe dactyloides*), and slim tridens (*Tridens muticus*). Adults nectar.

ABUNDANCE Uncommon; locally common in the west.

SEASON April to August.

Dotted Skipper
Hesperia attalus

UPPERSIDE

UNDERSIDE

SIZE 1⅜–1⅝ inches.

DESCRIPTION Uppersides are brown with dull orange spots and forewing center patch (males) or with pale spots (females). Males have a long thin black stigma. Underside is olive-brown to orange-brown with several small pale hindwing spots forming a post-median band plus one or two basal spots. Underwing spots may be small or missing.

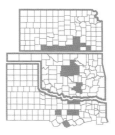

SIMILAR SPECIES Green Skipper has much larger underwing spots. Leonard's Skipper (not illustrated) is similar but flies much later in the year, has an orange to rust underside, and normally has larger underwing spots.

HABITAT Shortgrass prairies, oak savannas, and grassy openings in dry woods.

MAJOR FOOD PLANTS Caterpillars feed on plants in the grass family (Graminae), including sideoats grama (*Bouteloua curtipendula*), fall witchgrass (*Leptoloma cognatum*), and fall switchgrass (*Panicum virgatum*).

ABUNDANCE Uncommon.

SEASON May to September.

Tawny-edged Skipper

Polites themistocles

UPPERSIDE MALE

UPPERSIDE FEMALE

UNDERSIDE

SIZE ⅞–1⁷⁄₁₆ inches

DESCRIPTION Upperside is dark brown with an orange leading edge to the forewing and a few orange spots. Males have a long thin black stigma on the forewing. Underside of hindwing is brassy, normally with no markings. Some individuals have a postmedian band of light spots on the hindwing.

SIMILAR SPECIES Quite similar to Crossline Skipper, which is generally orange-brown below, presenting less contrast with the orange leading edge of the forewing. Most Crossline Skippers have a postmedian hindwing spot band. Note pale square spot on the forewing of female Crossline Skippers. Some Crossline Skippers have a brassier than normal underside with a reduced postmedian spot band—these individuals are difficult to differentiate from Tawny-edged Skipper.

HABITAT Prairies, fields, roadsides, weedy or grassy lots, and lawns.

MAJOR FOOD PLANTS Caterpillars feed on plants in the grass family (Graminae), including panic grasses (*Panicum*), slender crabgrass (*Digitaria filiformis*), and bluegrass (*Poa pratensis*). Adults nectar.

ABUNDANCE Common.

SEASON April to October.

Crossline Skipper

Polites origenes

UPPERSIDE MALE

UNDERSIDE

SIZE 1⅛–1½ inches.

DESCRIPTION Males are dark brown above with an orange leading edge and base to the forewing. Females are similar but have a much reduced or absent orange leading edge and have a pale square spot below the end of the cell. Males have a long dark forewing stigma. Underside of hindwing is orange-brown with a faint postmedian band of pale spots.

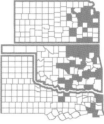

SIMILAR SPECIES Quite similar to Tawny-edged Skipper, which generally has a brassy underside contrasting well with the orange leading edge of the forewing. Most Tawny-edged Skippers do not have a distinctive postmedian hindwing spot band. Note orange leading edge and lack of black stigma on female Tawny-edged Skippers. Some Tawny-edged Skippers have a pronounced postmedian spot band; these individuals usually have the brassy underwings typical of the species but may still be difficult to differentiate from Crossline Skippers.

HABITAT Prairies, fields, roadsides, weedy or grassy lots, lawns, and grassy openings in woods and scrub.

MAJOR FOOD PLANTS Caterpillars feed on plants in the grass family (Graminae), including purpletop (*Tridens flavus*) and little bluestem (*Schizachyrium scoparius*).

ABUNDANCE Common.

SEASON May to September.

Southern Broken-Dash

Wallengrenia otho

UPPERSIDE MALE

UPPERSIDE FEMALE

UNDERSIDE

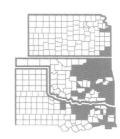

SIZE 1–1⅜ inches.

DESCRIPTION Males are brown on the upperside with a dark orange to rust leading edge to the forewing and similarly colored spots on the forewing apex and patch on the hindwing. The forewing also has an elongated black stigma separated into two parts. Females are dark brown above with pale yellow to orange spots on the forewing. Underside of hindwing in both sexes is dark orange to rust with a curved band of pale spots, usually shaped like a 3.

SIMILAR SPECIES The dark orange to rust color in combination with the 3-shaped band of pale spots separates this species from other skippers.

HABITAT Woodland or swamp openings and edges.

MAJOR FOOD PLANTS Caterpillars feed on plants in the grass family (Graminae), including paspalum (*Paspalum*) and hairy crabgrass (*Digitaria sanguinalis*).

ABUNDANCE Common.

SEASON May to September.

COMMENTS The broken-dash is named for the two-part stigma.

Sachem

Atalopedes campestris

UPPERSIDE MALE

UNDERSIDE MALE

UPPERSIDE FEMALE

UNDERSIDE FEMALE

SIZE 1 ¼–1 ⅝ inches.

DESCRIPTION Males are yellow-orange on the upperside with wide brown margins and a distinctively large oval-shaped black stigma. Underside is dull brown to orangish with a pale arrow-shaped band on the hindwing. Females are yellow-brown to dark brown above with two squarish transparent white spots at the end of the forewing cell and a

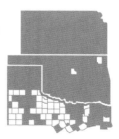

black patch basal to the transparent spots. Underside of hindwing is brown with an arrow-shaped band of pale spots.

SIMILAR SPECIES Sachems, especially when worn, often look like many other skippers. However, the large oval stigma of males is distinctive. Females are more problematic, but look for the transparent spots and associated black patch. When in doubt, the unknown skipper is probably a Sachem, as they are usually abundant.

HABITAT Disturbed, open areas, including weedy fields, roadsides, fields, gardens, and lawns.

MAJOR FOOD PLANTS Caterpillars feed on plants in the grass family (Graminae), including Bermuda grass (*Cynodon dactylon*), hairy crabgrass (*Digitaria sanguinalis*), St. Augustine grass (*Stenotaphrum secundatum*), and goosegrass (*Eleusine indica*).

ABUNDANCE Common to abundant.

SEASON April to November.

COMMENTS One of the most common butterflies in our area.

Arogos Skipper

Atrytone arogos

UNDERSIDE

SIZE 1⅛–1⁷⁄₁₆ inches.

DESCRIPTION Upperside is yellow-orange with wide black margins and whitish fringes; females have a wider black border and black streak in the center of the forewing. Underside of the hindwing of both sexes is yellow with paler veins.

SIMILAR SPECIES Could be confused with Delaware Skipper, which is more orange, has orange fringes, and has black veins on the forewings, especially toward the margins. Also similar to Byssus Skipper (not illustrated), which is larger, often has a light underwing patch or spot band in the center of the hindwing, and has black veins on the upperside.

HABITAT Requires high quality undisturbed grasslands and prairies.

MAJOR FOOD PLANTS Caterpillars feed on plants in the grass family (Graminae), including big bluestem (*Andropogon gerardii*), little bluestem (*Schizachyrium scoparius*), and possibly panic grass (*Panicum*). Adults nectar.

ABUNDANCE Locally common in high quality habitat only.

SEASON May to July.

COMMENTS Arogos Skippers are indicative of high quality prairie.

Delaware Skipper

Anatrytone logan

UPPERSIDE MALE

UPPERSIDE FEMALE

UNDERSIDE

SIZE 1–1¹¹⁄₁₆ inches.

DESCRIPTION Upperside is bright yellow-orange with black borders and black veins, especially near the margins. Forewings of females have wide black borders, a black spot at the base, and a black cell-end bar. Underside is bright yellow-orange with no markings.

SIMILAR SPECIES Could be confused with Arogos Skipper, which is more yellow and has whitish fringes but does not have black veins. Also similar to Byssus Skipper (not illustrated) which is larger, often has a pale underwing patch or spot band on the hindwing, and has more extensive black veining on the upperside.

HABITAT Moist brushy or grassy areas in prairies, fields, and roadsides. Occasionally wanders into yards.

MAJOR FOOD PLANTS Caterpillars feed on plants in the grass family (Graminae), including big bluestem (*Andropogon gerardii*) and fall switchgrass (*Panicum virgatum*). Adults nectar.
ABUNDANCE Uncommon.
SEASON May to August.

Zabulon Skipper

Poanes zabulon

UPPERSIDE MALE

UNDERSIDE MALE

UPPERSIDE FEMALE

UNDERSIDE FEMALE

SIZE 1⅜–1⅝ inches.

DESCRIPTION Males have bright yellow-orange uppersides with black borders and no stigma. Underside of hindwing is mostly yellow with dark brown wing base, outer margin, and scattered patches in the center. Females have brown uppersides with pale white to yellow spots. Underside of hindwing is brown with a white-edged apex, whitish gray marginal frosting, and lighter brown patterning in the center.

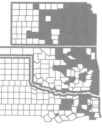

SIMILAR SPECIES Similar to Hobomok Skipper (not illustrated); but the male Hobomok Skipper has less yellow on the hindwing underside, and the female lacks the white-edged apex. Female Zabulon Skippers could be confused with worn Clouded Skippers or Dun Skippers, both of which either lack forewing spots or have smaller ones.

HABITAT Openings in moist woods.

MAJOR FOOD PLANTS Caterpillars feed on plants in the grass family (Graminae), including lovegrass (*Eragrostis*) and purpletop (*Tridens*).

ABUNDANCE Common.

SEASON May to September.

Dun Skipper

Euphyes vestris

UPPERSIDE MALE

UNDERSIDE MALE

UPPERSIDE FEMALE

UNDERSIDE FEMALE

SIZE 1⅛–1⅜ inches.

DESCRIPTION Both uppersides and undersides are medium to dark brown. Females have several subapical and central pale spots on the forewing. Males do not have spots but a black stigma may be visible. Upperside of head and thorax is often dark yellow-orange on males.

SIMILAR SPECIES Dun Skippers can be confused with worn Clouded Skippers, which are

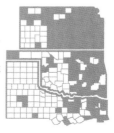

darker brown with light and dark patches on the hindwing underside. Female Zabulon and Hobomok (not illustrated) Skippers have larger white forewing spots than Clouded Skippers.

HABITAT Moist areas in or some distance from deciduous woods.

MAJOR FOOD PLANTS Caterpillars feed on plants in the sedge family (Cyperaceae), including yellow nutsedge (*Cyperus esculentus*) and other sedges (*Carex*).

ABUNDANCE Common.

SEASON April to October.

COMMENTS Fresh males may have a purplish cast on the underside.

Nysa Roadside-Skipper

Amblyscirtes nysa

UPPERSIDE

UNDERSIDE

SIZE ¾–1³⁄₁₆ inches.

DESCRIPTION Upperside is black with a few small submarginal white spots at the apex of the forewing. Fringe is checkered. Underside is dark brown mottled gray and black.

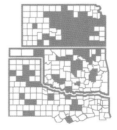

SIMILAR SPECIES Similar to other roadside-skippers, most of which are rare in our area except for Common Roadside-Skipper, which has an unmarked underwing with gray over-scaling at the forewing apex and outer half of the hindwing, and Bell's Roadside-Skipper, which has spots on the hindwing underside.

HABITAT Dry ravines, open areas in dry woods, fields, roadsides, and gardens.

MAJOR FOOD PLANTS Caterpillars feed on plants in the grass family (Graminae), including barnyard grass (*Echinochloa muricata*), St. Augustine grass (*Stenotaphrum secundatum*), hairy crab-grass (*Digitaria sanguinalis*), yellow foxtail (*Setaria glauca*), and paspalum (*Paspalum*).

ABUNDANCE Uncommon.

SEASON March to October.

Common Roadside-Skipper

Amblyscirtes vialis

UPPERSIDE

UNDERSIDE

SIZE ⅞–1¼ inches.

DESCRIPTION Upperside is black with a few small submarginal white spots at the apex of the forewing. Fringe is checkered. Underside is dark brown to black with grayish overscaling at the forewing apex and the outer half of the hindwing.

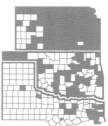

SIMILAR SPECIES Similar to other roadside-skippers, most of which are rare in our area, except for Nysa Roadside-Skipper, which has a mottled pattern to its underwings, and Bell's Roadside-Skipper which has spots on the hindwing underside.

HABITAT Openings in woods or scrub, often close to streams.

MAJOR FOOD PLANTS Caterpillars feed on plants in the grass family (Graminae), including inland seaoats (*Chasmanthium latifolium*), bentgrass (*Agrostis*), and bluegrass (*Poa*).

ABUNDANCE Common.

SEASON May to October.

Bell's Roadside-Skipper

Amblyscirtes belli

UPPERSIDE

UNDERSIDE

SIZE 1 ³⁄₁₆–1 ¼ inches.

DESCRIPTION Upperside is black with many small white spots on the forewing. Fringe is checkered. Underside is dark brown to black with numerous whitish spots and faint grayish overscaling on the hindwing (except for the hindwing apex).

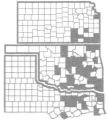

SIMILAR SPECIES Similar to other roadside-skippers, most of which are rare in our area except for Nysa Roadside-Skipper, which has a mottled pattern to its underwings, and Common Roadside-Skipper, which has an unmarked underwing with gray overscaling at the forewing apex and outer half of the hindwing.

HABITAT Openings in dry woods and scrub, often near streams, and occasionally in gardens and parks.

MAJOR FOOD PLANTS Caterpillars feed on inland seaoats (*Chasmanthium latifolium*) in the grass family (Graminae).

ABUNDANCE Common.

SEASON Mid-April to September.

Eufala Skipper

Lerodea eufala

UPPERSIDE

UNDERSIDE

SIZE 1–1¼ inches.

DESCRIPTION Upperside is grayish brown with three to five small transparent spots on the forewing. Underside of hindwing is grayish brown, often unmarked but may have a faint spot band.

SIMILAR SPECIES This relatively nondescript species could be confused with the Ocola Skipper, which has elongated forewings and is

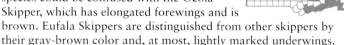

brown. Eufala Skippers are distinguished from other skippers by their gray-brown color and, at most, lightly marked underwings.

HABITAT Weedy places, roadsides, lawns, and fields.

MAJOR FOOD PLANTS Caterpillars feed on plants in the grass family (Graminae), including Johnson grass (*Sorghum halapense*), Bermuda grass (*Cynodon dactylon*), barnyard grass (*Echinochloa crus-galli*), bristly foxtail (*Setaria verticillata*), corn (*Zea mays*), and rice (*Oryza sativa*).

ABUNDANCE Common.

SEASON June to October.

Ocola Skipper

Panoquina ocola

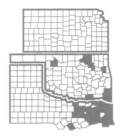

UNDERSIDE

SIZE 1³⁄₈–1¹¹⁄₁₆ inches.

DESCRIPTION Upperside is brown with five translucent spots on the forewing. Underside is brown. The forewing is long, extending far beyond the hindwing, and may have a postmedian line of whitish spots. The underside may have a purplish sheen when fresh. The abdomen has a dark line running along the side.

SIMILAR SPECIES A fresh Ocola Skipper is distinctive. Worn Ocola Skippers may be confused with other brown skippers except for the exceptionally long forewings.

HABITAT Fields, open pine woodlands, and gardens.

MAJOR FOOD PLANTS Caterpillars feed on rice (*Oryza sativa*) and other aquatic and semiaquatic grasses in the grass family (Graminae). Adults nectar.

ABUNDANCE Generally an uncommon stray from the south but may be common in some years and locations.

SEASON June to September.

Yucca Giant-Skipper

Megathymus yuccae

UPPERSIDE

UNDERSIDE

SIZE 1⅞–3⅛ inches.

DESCRIPTION A huge dark skipper. The upperside is black with a tan-yellow hindwing margin and yellowish and white spots on the forewing. The underside is also black, with white frosting on the edges of both wings and a large white spot near the leading edge of the forewing.

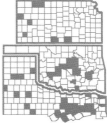

SIMILAR SPECIES The size and coloring of this distinctive species prevent confusion with all other skippers except for Strecker's Giant-Skipper (not illustrated), which flies later in the year, is grayish, and has white spots on the hindwing underside.

HABITAT Grasslands, scrub, and open woodlands with yucca.

MAJOR FOOD PLANTS Caterpillars feed on most species in the yucca family (Agavaceae) in the United States, including *Yucca arkansana*, *Y. glauca*, and *Y. neomexicana*. Adults do not nectar. Adult males sip mud; females do not feed.

ABUNDANCE Rare to locally common.

SEASON March to May.

COMMENTS This impressive butterfly is a treat to find and watch.

PART 2

Butterflies at Home and in Nature

Life Stages and
Raising Butterflies

Butterflies have been on earth more than 100 million years, much longer than we have. In Colorado, fossils have been found of butterflies that existed 48 million years ago. No doubt, ancient species were flying in the southern plains at this time. From carvings and paintings depicting butterflies, we know that early cultures throughout the world appreciated butterfly form and colors, and our admiration has continued through the centuries. One expression of this fascination is a growing interest in raising butterflies to observe and understand their life history.

By rearing butterflies in a protected environment, you not only enhance their survival rate—you provide rewarding experiences for yourself. Having access to butterfly life stages offers many photography opportunities, and keeping meticulous records allows you to learn more about the natural history of these insects and share this information with others. Perhaps most important, raising butterflies has the potential to teach young people valuable lessons: exposure to the complex inter-relationships found in nature kindles curiosity and concern for the natural world. Clarence Weed stated in his 1926 book *Butterflies*: "There are few things in the world more interesting to watch than the wonderful changes which a moth or butterfly goes through in the course of its life" (43–44).

Enclosure

The first step is to select a suitable enclosure. Butterflies have been reared in jars, shoe boxes, cardboard boxes, and plastic containers. To succeed, the enclosure must: (1) allow in fresh air, (2) keep caterpillars contained, (3) prevent entry of predators and parasitoid wasps and flies, (4) have correct temperature requirements, neither too warm nor too cold, and (5) permit easy access to clean the interior and replace host plants.

If a large host plant is available in a flower pot or yard, a section of the plant can be surrounded with garden netting and closed at the base to keep larvae (caterpillars) within the safety of the netting. As a section of the plant is defoliated, the remainder can be pruned and transferred with the clinging caterpillars to a fresh area of the host plant and reshrouded.

However, you may want to consider the purchase of a cage specifically designed for raising butterflies and other invertebrates to observe the butterfly's life stages clearly and to provide the best possible chances of survival. Companies that specialize in entomology-related products carry rearing cages ranging from small collapsible metal units costing approximately $35 to large walk-in enclosures at more than $400.

A rearing cage can be easily and economically built for $12 to $14 from materials purchased at a home-improvement store (fig. 1.1). A convenient size is a 12 x 12 x 12 in. cage made of ¾ x ¾ in. white pine. After purchasing 12 ft. of wood ($6 to $7), saw it into 12 in. sections. Nail the frame together with 1¼ in. nails and reinforce the joints with a high quality wood glue. After the glue has dried, cover the cage with a screen. Fiberglass insect screen can be purchased in a 3 x 6 ft. roll ($4 to $5) in a gray color for easy viewing. Cut the screening into six sections of appropriate size to cover the exterior of the cage. Carefully staple each section to the sides and bottom of the cage, using staples no larger than ¼ in. First instar caterpillars are tiny and can easily escape if all openings are not closed. The top section of screen should be cut oversized and simply laid on top of the cage with the corners weighted, allowing for easy access to the interior. Pebbles or small flat shards from broken flower pots work well as weights. Weights should not be large enough to injure a caterpillar or chrysalis if they happen to fall inside the cage or to prevent adequate light or ventilation.

FIG. 1.1. An inexpensive homemade
rearing cage for raising butterflies.

Obtaining Eggs and Caterpillars

Having a butterfly garden with both nectar and host plants will make it easy to locate eggs and caterpillars as well as providing ample supplies of host plants for larval consumption (see Species Accounts for information on butterfly host plants). Butterfly eggs are tiny, usually less than ¹⁄₁₆ of an inch (fig. 1.2). They vary in size, color, and shape, depending on species. Females often lay eggs on the underside of host leaves. After verifying the suitability of the plant through vision and chemical receptors in their antennae, some females "taste" the plant with chemical receptors located at the bottom of their legs. Eggs can also be found on host plant stems, buds, and tops and tips of leaves. Some species place their eggs near rather than on a host. Eggs take approximately five days to hatch; however, the period is variable.

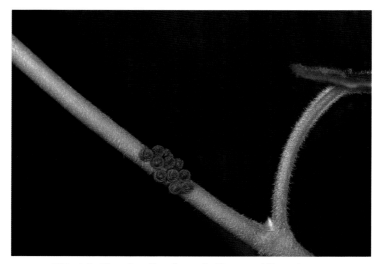

FIG. 1.2. Pipevine Swallowtail *(Battus philenor)* eggs.

FIG. 1.3. Black Swallowtail *(Papilio polyxenes)* caterpillar.
Note the protruding orange osmaterium.

Caterpillars (fig. 1.3) are also frequently found on the underside of leaves, where they gain some protection from inclement weather and predators. Caterpillars are often difficult to find since they remain immobile much of the time. The larvae of many species have evolved to resemble something other than caterpillars. The Black Swallowtail (*Papilio polyxenes*), for example, looks like a small bird dropping in its early instars. Butterfly caterpillars cannot grow without molting their exoskeleton or outer skin, and each stage of growth is called an instar. Many species blend into the background through the use of countershading and cryptic coloration. When looking for a well-camouflaged species such as a fourth or fifth instar Black Swallowtail on fennel, dill, or parsley, changing the angle of view can sometimes reveal a caterpillar that was previously invisible. Wasps, with persistent searching, seem to have a high success rate in locating caterpillars, but they are using other senses in addition to vision.

Some species take refuge in a folded or tented leaf shelter, sewn together with silk. A common species in our area, the Silver-spotted Skipper (*Epargyreus clarus*), shelters in a folded leaf when very young but pulls several leaves together to form a tent in later instars. Most caterpillars are solitary, although some, such as the Pipevine Swallowtail, are social feeders in early instars, and you may find ten or more together.

Do not brush against the host plants since caterpillars, as a defense measure, often immediately release their hold if the host is bumped and drop to the ground. Unlike butterfly adults, caterpillars have poor vision. Research and personal observation reveal that the caterpillars frequently cannot find their way back onto the host plant and will not survive.

By taking the early stages of a butterfly into a rearing cage and caring for them properly, you increase the individual's chance of surviving the many dangers it would face in the natural world from parasitoids, predators, and human activity. Only a small fraction of caterpillars reach adulthood. However, placing too many eggs or caterpillars into the rearing cage may result in overcrowding, disease, and other problems.

Always use local eggs and caterpillars for rearing. The practice of obtaining butterflies by mail order is fraught with danger for butterflies. Imported butterflies can introduce disease into local populations and compromise the genetic integrity of local species and subspecies. Importing butterflies makes it difficult for lepidopterists to evaluate population numbers, fluctuations, and species ranges—all necessary information when establishing conservation strategies. One major concern is the possibility of introducing an alien species that might outcompete native butterflies.

Care

After eclosing (hatching) through one end of the egg, the caterpillar often eats all or part of the egg shell as its first meal. It will then nibble on its host plant. Initially, you may be replacing wilted leaves with fresh ones, but take care to not throw the caterpillar away. Host plant cuttings can be placed in a small-mouth vase or jar filled with water to keep the plant material fresh. The top should be closed off with plastic wrap so that caterpillars cannot stray into the container and drown. Rinse the host plant with water before feeding because your neighbor may use herbicides and/or pesticides that could drift onto your property. A small amount of moisture on the plant can also prevent the young caterpillars from desiccating. Inspect the leaves to ensure that you are not accidentally introducing an ant, assassin bug, praying mantis, spider, or other predator into the cage. These animals should be released unharmed as they are vital to keeping balances in the natural world. Also, look for additional butterfly eggs or caterpillars on host plants before removing the leaves or plant from the garden, unless you have additional cages for newcomers. Otherwise, the additional caterpillars will have to fend for themselves and are less likely to survive.

Caterpillars void waste in the form of small pellets called frass. Clean paper towels should be placed in the bottom of the cage as needed to avoid disease and to ensure healthy butterflies. After the first instar, the paper towels should be changed daily and progressively more often as the caterpillars mature. When cleaning a cage containing early instar caterpillars, place the old host plant on a clean paper towel outside the cage so that any tiny caterpillars dropping off it can be seen. Do not handle them as they are easily injured. Caterpillars can be recovered by allowing them to crawl onto a fresh sprig of plant material, or you can use featherweight forceps to place them gently on the plant. Count the caterpillars before closing the cage.

When rearing a swallowtail butterfly, note the reaction when it feels threatened. The caterpillar may produce a brightly colored forked organ at the front of the thorax, called an osmaterium (fig. 1.3). This organ emits a chemical to repel predators. The odor of the substance has been described as foul, but some people do not find it unpleasant.

A caterpillar progresses through four or more stages of growth or instars. The number varies with species; five instars are common. The caterpillars not only change size but can also change shape and color. At the end of each instar, the caterpillar often has a shiny look and becomes lethargic. It may temporarily leave the host plant to shed its skin (called ecdysis). The discarded, wrinkled exoskeleton and head capsule can sometimes be found in the bottom of the cage.

In later instars, caterpillars consume prodigious amounts of food. On quiet evenings it is possible to hear leaf tearing sounds coming from the cages. At this time, your housekeeping and food providing chores increase significantly. Butterfly caterpillars and pupae are vulnerable to various diseases if cages are overcrowded and not keep scrupulously clean. They can be attacked by fungi and bacteria, but the most common threat is from the polyhedrosis viruses. An infected caterpillar or pupa will darken and eventually turn black while oozing a foul-smelling fluid. When the cage is empty at the end of the rearing season, clean it with soap and water or a bleach solution (one part bleach added to ten parts water). Thoroughly rinse with water after cleaning. Note that cages may not be empty until the following spring for species that overwinter in the larval or pupal stage before adulthood.

When the caterpillars reach their fourth or fifth instar, a few twigs should be added to the cage, as it is more convenient for you if the caterpillar pupates on a twig rather than on the side or top of the cage. Pupation occurs when the caterpillar metamorphoses into a chrysalis (pupa), the stage before the adult butterfly (fig. 1.4). When caterpillars are ready to pupate—which may be two or three weeks after the egg is laid, depending on a number of factors, such as species, temperature, and humidity—they move rapidly around the cage looking for an appropriate site. A dormant period follows, which can last 24 hours or longer. Some species pupate inside a leaf shelter, or the pupa may be found in leaf and grass debris. Others spin a silken pad and button from which they suspend themselves. The next developmental step is critical. The larval skin splits apart at predetermined, weakened lines of fracture, and the caterpillar struggles free of its final skin and suspends itself by inserting hooks at the end of the abdomen, called a cremaster, into the silk button. Some species also gain additional support from a silken thread or girdle that loops around the midregion of the chrysalis.

The chrysalis may hang for a week or longer, depending on the species, temperature, weather, and time of year. The butterfly may sense poor weather and will rarely eclose until conditions improve. Some species enter diapause, or slow down their development, for the winter. The only care they will need is to be placed in a protected area, like an unheated garage, and lightly misted with water periodically. Do not bring pupae into the house or a heated area, as they will eclose before nectar and host plants are available.

Some pupae wiggle if disturbed, but most of the time they are quiescent, at least on the exterior. Within the chrysalis a miraculous transformation is taking place. You can sometimes

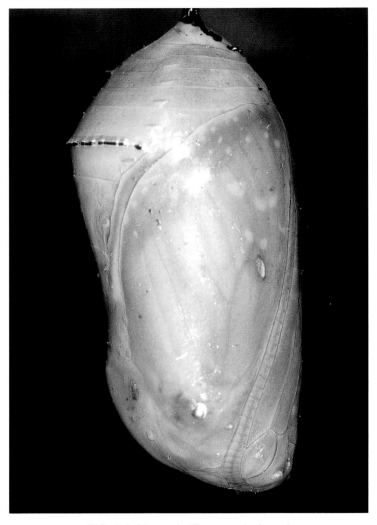

FIG. 1.4. Monarch *(Danaus plexippus)*
chrysalis nearing eclosure.

see the butterfly within the pupa when it is nearing eclosure or emergence (fig. 1.4). Eclosure is often in the morning. The chrysalis splits apart near the head and the butterfly struggles out of its pupal shell. The adult stage is called the imago.

At this time you may want to take the opportunity to observe the three parts of an insect: the head, the thorax, and the abdomen (figs. 1.5, 1.6). The four wings and six legs are attached to the thorax. Although butterflies are sometimes described as being cold-blooded animals, they are actually ectotherms that need an ambient temperature of about 60°F and the heat of sunlight to warm their thoracic muscles to operate the legs and wings.

A fascinating part of butterfly behavior is thermoregulation or the steps a butterfly takes to regulate its temperature.

FIG. 1.5. Monarch *(Danaus plexippus)* butterfly showing three body segments while basking.

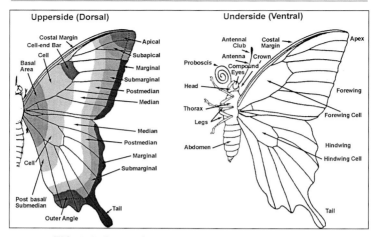

FIG. 1.6. Parts of a butterfly and typical wing areas.

Butterflies often bask in sunlight as the thorax must have a temperature of approximately 80°F for the butterfly to attain efficient flight. They use various basking positions; the most common are dorsal basking, with wings spread open while angled horizontal to the sun, and lateral basking, with the wings vertical and angled perpendicular to the sun. Some species rapidly quiver or "shiver" their wings to elevate the thoracic temperature. This enables them to use their legs to walk to a sunny area to bask. Of course, excessive heat can be dangerous, and butterflies will take appropriate measures to avoid overheating by cooling off in the shade or adjusting their wings to shield the abdomen and thorax from the sun.

Although thermoregulation is a daily concern for butterflies that have emerged from the chrysalis, other tasks must be dealt with immediately after eclosure during what is called the teneral period. During this period the imago pumps fluid into its wings while allowing them to hang and dry. The butterfly repeatedly coils and uncoils its proboscis as it attempts to join the two halves of this vital organ together, and it flexes its wings from time to time. The butterfly needs a safe place to hang after eclosure as it is helpless and the wings are easily damaged or deformed if disturbed.

The teneral period may last several hours. Then with a silent flap of the wings, the always thrilling first flight takes place. The presence of a butterfly garden with nectar and host plants will encourage the return of these "frail children of the air" (Scudder, 1895), and the cycle will start anew.

2

Butterfly Survival

Considering the many hazards that butterflies must overcome at each stage of their lives, it seems unfair that they should have such a brief life span as adults. Most live only few days to a few weeks in their most elegant and ornamental life stage. However, their transitory beauty is an asset when it comes to trying to ensure their conservation in a world where human-induced problems compound the natural hazards they already face. There is much that is interesting and much that remains mysterious about butterfly survival.

A short adult period may be all that is necessary for most butterfly species, as the primary role of the adult is to find a mate, breed, locate an appropriate host plant for its young, and deposit eggs, acquiring along the way only enough nourishment to sustain itself until these tasks are accomplished. Exceptions occur, including the Mourning Cloak (*Nymphalis antiopa*), which overwinters as an adult and may live up to ten months. The final summer generation of the Monarch (*Danaus plexippus*) makes a long migratory journey in the fall and can live until the following spring, perhaps seven to eight months, although later generations of Monarchs may live only one month.

Reproduction

Butterfly mating can involve species-specific flight and perching behavior as well as the dissemination of pheromones or scented chemicals to facilitate the process. Pheromones may come from specialized scales on the wings called androconial scales. Sometimes these scales are quite obvious and aid the observer in identifying not only the species but the sex of the butterfly. Skippers of one group are called branded skippers (grass-skippers) because of the stigma, a highly visible concentration of specialized androconial scales on the male's forewing.

In some species, males eclose from the chrysalis before the females. This phenomenon is called protandry and allows the male to establish a territory or vantage point in anticipation of female arrival. Males may employ a perch-and-wait strategy, patrol a territory, or frequent a hilltop (known as hilltopping) in search of females. Encounters may also occur at nectar sites. Males of some species expedite the reproductive process by mating with a female before, during, or shortly after her emergence from the chrysalis (fig. 2.1). At other times the female can reject a male's advances by fluttering her wings while elevating her abdomen in a "rejection posture." Females may take flight if males continue to harasses them.

Successful mating involves the passing of a sperm packet called a spermatophore from the male to the female (fig. 2.2). The spermatophore fertilizes the eggs and also provides nutrition for the female. The spermatophore enters the egg through the micropyle. Mating can last from less than an hour to several hours. If disturbed, the joined butterflies may take flight with one butterfly carrying the other. Which sex carries the other varies, depending on the species.

FIG. 2.1. Gulf Fritillaries *(Agraulis vanillae)* mating on chrysalis.

FIG. 2.2. Variegated Fritillaries *(Euptoieta claudia)* mating.

Survival in the Natural World

Kansas, Oklahoma, and North Texas are subject to sudden and extreme changes in weather that can present many problems for butterflies. A late spring or too much or too little rainfall can adversely affect the availability of host plants and nectar plants, resulting in a paucity of butterflies. However, fluctuations in butterfly numbers due to weather are normal, and many species rebound when host and nectar plants recover.

Observers have experienced how sensitive butterflies are to sunlight. A flowering meadow or garden can be teeming with nectaring butterflies that quickly vanish with the arrival of clouds and the possibility of rain, as the butterflies seek refuge under leaves, grass, or some other shelter until the sunlight returns.

Butterflies use a variety of strategies to deal with adverse weather. Small species such as the Eastern Tailed-Blue (*Everes comyntas*) fly close to the ground, where the air temperature is warmer and there is less buffeting on windy days. During the warmest summer months, some species such as the Mourning Cloak estivate or become dormant until fall when they again become active. Large butterflies such as the Pipevine Swallowtail (*Battus philenor*) retreat from the summer heat to a shaded area or close their wings to prevent the thorax from overheating.

Butterflies can be flexible and may be able to learn new behavior patterns that can aid survival. Some adult members of the genus *Heliconius* prolong their lives by extracting and ingesting pollen, a source of nitrogen, in addition to using nectar. The Zebra Heliconian (*Heliconius charithonia*), which strays into our area from Mexico and South Texas, can live up to 4½ months using this specialized diet. The female is able to oviposit throughout most of her life as long as she has access to pollen. Survival may also be enhanced by roosting in groups in the evenings, which may confront predators with a large number of aposematic butterflies (showing warning colors). In addition, the group can detect the approach of a predator better by having many eyes on the alert. The Zebra Heliconian seems to have the ability to learn. A night roost leads to recruitment of new members, which follow older members back to the roosting site in the evening. The next day the newest arrivals follow the experienced butterflies as they "trapline" or make the rounds to known nectar and pollen sources, thus learning the location of those resources.

Some species, such as the Long-tailed Skipper (*Urbanus proteus*), immigrate into our area to exploit available resources. Another strong flier from the south, the Brazilian Skipper (*Calpodes ethlius*), has been recorded in our area. Other butterflies that cannot survive our winter but migrate into the area each summer from Mexico include the Cloudless Sulphur (*Phoebis sennae*) and the Painted Lady (*Vanessa cardui*). Of course, the best known migrating butterfly is the Monarch, which leaves its Mexican winter home in March. Succeeding generations move north, exploiting the emerging milkweed. Many enter Canada, several generations removed from the Monarch of the early spring. The final brood makes the long journey of up to 2,000 miles back to central Mexico in the fall.

Butterflies have many predators. Although the ability to fly and to detect movement lessens the threat of terrestrial predators such as mice, frogs, anoles, lizards, and spiders, butterflies are at risk from these species when resting. They must also deal with more formidable winged predators, including birds and some insects. Birds such as flycatchers are proficient at "hawking" insects from the air. One author observed a Great Crested Flycatcher take a fluttering Hackberry Emperor (*Asterocampa celtis*). Robber flies and dragonflies attack insects on the wing from three to twelve feet away. Some butterflies, such as the Regal Fritillary (*Speyeria idalia*), have strong flight muscles and are powerful fliers; with a quick burst of speed they can elude a bird. Predators may learn to avoid Regal Fritillaries so as not to waste energy on unsuccessful attempts. The Zebra Swallowtail (*Eurytides marcellus*), found in eastern Kansas, Oklahoma, and North Texas, has a wing pattern that is disruptive, breaking up the form of the butterfly and confusing the predator.

Butterflies may use cryptic coloration (crypsis) in all life stages to conceal themselves from enemies. The adult Mourning Cloak, Question Mark (*Polygonia interrogationis*), Eastern Comma (*P. comma*), and Goatweed Leafwing (*Anaea andria*) all have predominantly brown or gray surfaces on the underside of both forewing and hindwing, camouflaging the animal when it is perched with closed wings on bark or soil. Some species have drab undersides and routinely perch with wings closed to blend with the background, but if discovered, they quickly open their wings to expose a bright upper surface, which may have eyespots that add to the "startle effect." If the predator hesitates, the butterfly may escape. Even species with relatively muted colors, such as the Common Wood-Nymph (*Cercyonis pegala*), may benefit from eyespots in a similar manner.

The hairstreaks are small butterflies that perch with wings closed so that the center of attraction is the bright spot at the rear or anal angle of the hindwing. Streaks, lines, or small spots often lead the eye to this area. One or two hairlike tails resembling antennae attached to the hindwing may cause a predator to focus on this area of the wing for an attack, believing it is attacking the head of its prey. This so-called "false-head" effect is heightened by the butterfly rubbing its hindwings together while it is perched or nectaring, drawing the attack to a less vulnerable part of its anatomy, as a small part of the wing will tear away when grasped, and the target may escape. Butterflies with portions of the hindwing missing, sometimes in the V shape of a beak, are often seen in the field. When tailed butterflies land, they sometimes quickly reverse their position to present the tail where the head was initially located. Interestingly, the Coral Hairstreak (*Satyrium titus*) does not have tails, yet it also rubs the hindwings together while perched. Groups of butterflies other than hairstreaks include species with tails such as the ubiquitous Eastern Tailed-Blue.

Some butterflies, notably the Pipevine Swallowtail, Baltimore Checkerspot (*Euphydryas phaeton*), and Monarch, are aposematic or warningly colored. In the natural world orange or yellow with black often advertises that an animal is poisonous or unpalatable or emetic. Butterflies may sequester these poisons in the larval stage. For example, the Monarch obtains cardenolide heart poisons from its larval host, milkweed, although it does so with varying degrees of toxicity, depending on the species of milkweed. Even if the milkweed provides little or no heart-poison chemicals, a Monarch may gain protection from a bird's previous bad experience attempting to consume a Monarch that was richer in cardiac glycosides. The palatable Monarch thus gains protection from an unpalatable member of the same species, which is termed automimicry.

However, plant alkaloids sequestered in some butterfly species and the warning colors of mimicry do not seem to protect butterflies from many predacious insects and spiders. An assassin bug will readily attack a Monarch. Praying mantids and dragonflies are capable of taking large as well as small butterflies. Crab spiders lurk on the very flowers that butterflies use for life-giving nectar, and butterflies can be found entrapped in the webs of larger spiders. Ants attack all life stages of the butterfly. Paradoxically, some larvae of the family Lycaenidae are tended by ants in a relationship called myrmecophily, which increases the survival rate of the butterfly. For example, caterpillars of Edwards' Hairstreak (*Satyrium edwardsii*), found in eastern sections of our area, and Melissa Blue (*Lycaeides melissa*) in the western region are tended by ants and receive protection from parasites and predators in return for providing the ants with a sweet substance from abdominal glands.

Conservation

Butterflies have evolved a number of characteristics and behaviors for dealing with challenges found in the natural world. They have been so successful that they can be found in seemingly inhospitable environments on mountains and in arid regions. Butterflies occur on all continents but Antarctica.

Like many plants and other animals, butterflies are faced with habitat degradation, fragmentation, and loss caused by human disturbance. Habitat loss has occurred so rapidly that some species have become threatened or endangered, while others have been extirpated from areas of their former range. In California, the Xerces Blue (*Glaucopsyche xerces*) became extinct in 1943 because of human activity. In 1975, the first butterfly was placed on the United States Endangered Species List. No butterfly placed on this list has fully recovered. Unfortunately, up to 19 percent of butterfly species in the United States may be at risk.

An overall loss of habitat for some butterfly species will likely come with the increased rate of global warming predicted for this century. Although butterflies have always had to deal with climate changes, the change attributed to greenhouse gas emissions will likely be rapid. Some species may expand their range northward. For example, the Edith's Checkerspot (*Euphydryas editha*) in California has expanded its range northward and to higher elevations, yet at the same time populations at lower elevations or in the south have been extirpated. Research on European butterflies indicates that 22 of 35 species examined have shifted their ranges northward during the 20th century. However, many species are sedentary and others, including montane and migratory species, are restricted in their movement by a lack of host plants or are limited by other ecological constraints. These species will be particularly vulnerable to climate change.

Species with specialized ecological requirements are restricted to specific types of habitat and are highly vulnerable to habitat loss. Pollution or draining of wetlands led to a decline in Bronze Coppers (*Lycaena hyllus*), a butterfly found in Kansas and northern Oklahoma. The loss of prairie through conversion to farmland or development has led to the decline and extirpation of the Arogos Skipper (*Atrytone arogos*) from much of its former range in the east. The Frosted Elfin (*Callphrys irus*), another species declining in parts of the East and Midwest, can be found in local populations in woodland edges and openings of southeast Oklahoma and East Texas. Not only must these openings be maintained by periodic fire or other disturbance, but corridors are necessary to allow dispersal among populations and avoid the loss of genetic fitness that comes with isolation and too small a population. Without undisturbed hilly and mountainous forest habitat, the Diana Fritillary (*Speyeria diana*) of eastern Oklahoma, a butterfly that lepidopterist William H. Howe has described as "the loveliest of the genus," will be lost.

The most recognizable butterfly in our area, the Monarch, is now beset with problems in both its winter and summer homes. These threats are serious enough to cause some lepidopterists to declare the spectacular migration of the Monarch to be an "endangered phenomenon." Much of the area in the Transverse Neovolcanic Belt of central Mexico, where the eastern population of the Monarch winters, was set aside as preserves by the government of Mexico. However, failure to execute protective measures has led to thinning and destruction of the vital fir forest cover through logging and agrarian interests. Buffer areas have also deteriorated. In the United States, the reliance of agriculture on pesticides, herbicides, biological control of exotics, and more recently on growing corn that has been genetically modified with the bacterium *Bacillus thuringiensis* (Bt) can cause problems for the Monarch in an important part of its breeding range. Pollen from Bt modified corn can be wind dispersed onto milkweed being consumed by larvae in adjoining fields. This could have a detrimental effect on the larvae of other species as well.

Restoration of habitat does not automatically mean protection of butterflies or the recovery of extirpated species, as there may be no butterflies to take advantage of the restored area. Evaluating the health of a butterfly population or the effectiveness of recovery plans involves complex ecological considerations. Natural fluctuations in butterfly numbers must be accurately gauged to determine if a species is in trouble. Studies are labor intensive, require many hours of field work, and can be expensive. Lepidopterists should be included in both conservation planning and monitoring of the effectiveness of recovery measures.

The Regal Fritillary has been in recognizable trouble since the 1970s, yet continued to decline throughout much of its range. Even when protected prairies were allowed to recover from overgrazing and the use of herbicides, the Regal Fritillary was still missing from some areas. A healthy prairie requires fire, but Regal Fritillaries overwinter as minute first instar larvae that cannot survive spring burns. Frequent prescribed burning over too large an area results in spectacular plant growth but destroys invertebrates. Controlled burning over small sections of a prairie on a rotating basis, about every six years, is less destructive. Mowing on a rotating basis would be even more beneficial for butterflies. Even though the Regal Fritillary is a strong flier and can disperse over a great distance, it is still declining, indicating that recovery may involve other difficult questions such as preserve size, specific larval host plant requirements, and adult nectar requirements.

Other factors that can increase the difficulty of protecting butterfly populations are host plant preferences, propensity to travel distances, and symbiotic relationships. Some butterfly species are monophagous, meaning that larvae use only a single species of plant host, or oligophagous, with larvae feeding on a few closely related plants in the same family. For example, Great Purple Hairstreak (*Atlides halesus*) caterpillars only feed on mistletoe. Luckily, mistletoe is common, or else this spectacular butterfly would be much rarer. Other species do not travel far from their preferred habitats and may be restricted to small areas if their habitat is limited. For example, the Arogos Skipper requires high quality tallgrass prairie and is rare away from selected sites. Some butterfly species have symbiotic relationships with a limited number of ant species and are therefore confined to particular soil types where these ants occur. Combinations of factors such as limited host plant preference, inability to travel, and/or a rare host plant can reduce the population of a butterfly species and can complicate recovery from population lows. Viable populations with all parts of their ecosystem intact are the easiest to protect. A declining or endangered species may be difficult to save if the recovery plan must include a great number of complex problems involving the requirements of a particular species as well as the restoration of ecological relationships.

It is our hope that greater appreciation of butterflies will lead to concern for their conservation. Since butterflies can be indicators of a healthy ecosystem, their protection can only improve environmental conditions. Those concerned about the future of lepidoptera recognize that there are serious problems. With perseverance, all of these problems can be solved. A start would be to join organizations such as the North American Butterfly Association and the Xerces Society, which have the conservation of butterflies as a primary goal. The Nature Conservancy is an organization that acquires critical habitat for protection, and these efforts should also be supported (see Organizations and Resources at the back of the book).

To assist butterflies directly, we can follow the lead of the great 20th-century British statesman Winston Churchill. He planted butterfly gardens at Chartwell, his estate in Kent, and also maintained a shelter to raise butterflies for release into his gardens. In 1948–49, Churchill took the extraordinary step of attempting the reintroduction of the Black-veined White (*Aporia crataegi*), a butterfly that had been extirpated from Britain between 1912 and 1925, some believe due to pesticide spraying in orchards. While most of us do not have access to a country estate for planting our own butterfly gardens, success can come from something as modest as a window box or a patio garden. In the next chapter we explain how to create a garden to benefit butterflies as well as providing hours of pleasure for the gardener.

Butterfly Gardening

Few things are more beautiful than a garden filled with bright flowers and alive with the movement and color of butterflies. Butterflies can be found virtually anywhere, even in downtown Dallas, Oklahoma City, or Wichita. A well-planned garden can maximize the number of butterflies and increase the enjoyment of your urban or rural property. While most butterflies observed are common species, an occasional rare visitor can make butterfly gardens a prime location for butterfly watching. The greatest number of butterfly species will occur if your garden is next to an abandoned field, woodlot, prairie, marsh, or other natural area. Your plantings will draw in species that may normally be found only in areas less disturbed than a typical garden.

The key points for a butterfly garden include:
1. Nectar plants for adults.
2. Host plants for caterpillars.
3. A diverse selection of plant materials, especially native plants.
4. A predominantly sunny and sheltered location.
5. Minimal insecticide use.
6. Miscellaneous elements such as leaf litter ground cover, wood pile, rotting fruit, and damp ground.

Nectar Plants

The adults of most species of butterflies feed on nectar from flowers (fig. 3.1). Many species of flowers provide both beauty and nectar for butterflies. Butterfly-pollinated plants tend to have numerous small flowers grouped in a cluster, as seen with lantana, or surrounded by a landing platform of large petals as found on coneflower and Indian blanket. Large butterflies such as swallowtails and fritillaries tend to prefer tall flowers. Low-growing flowers are often frequented by small, low-flying butterflies. Some species, such as Dun Skipper (*Euphyes vestris*), Dion Skipper (*E. dion*), and Clouded Skipper (*Lerema accius*) also tend to fly to low plants for refuge when they feel threatened. Some prime native and nonnative plants to consider as nectar sources are listed in tables 3.1 and 3.2.

If you have limited space for a butterfly garden, it may be best to focus on nectar plants. A couple of containers of lantana and pentas on an apartment balcony can be enough to draw in a few butterflies. Even a lone butterfly bush in a planter surrounded by concrete or a small patch of mistflower along a drainage ditch can be covered with butterflies. When working with small spaces, create miniature gardens by using plants of several species. Many of the common nectar plants are very drought and heat tolerant and work well in tight spaces.

Caterpillar Plants

To maintain a healthy population of butterflies in or near a garden, we need to provide host plants upon which the caterpillars can feed (fig. 3.2). Many of the most common garden butterflies are those species in which the caterpillars feed on a wide range of plants—Eastern Tiger Swallowtail (*Papilio glaucus*), Cabbage White (*Pieris rapae*), Gray Hairstreak (*Strymon melinus*), Eastern Tailed-Blue (*Everes comyntas*), Pearl Crescent (*Phyciodes tharos*),

FIG. 3.1. American Lady *(Vanessa virginiensis)* nectaring on flower.

Question Mark (*Polygonia interrogationis*), Common Buckeye (*Junonia coenia*), and Sachem (*Atalopedes campestris*). Other butterflies prefer only a limited number of host plant species but can be abundant if the proper host plants are in the garden

Table 3.1 Easily cultivated native species that are heavily used nectar sources

Name	Plant type	Flower color	Flowering season	Height
Butterfly weed (*Asclepias tuberosa*)	perennial	orange to yellow	mid-May to July	1–2.5 ft.
Perennial asters (*Aster*)	perennial	white, pink, purple	July to Oct.	1–4 ft.
Buttonbush (*Cephalanthus occidentalis*)	shrub	white	June to July	4–10 ft.
Purple coneflower (*Echinacea purpurea*)	perennial	purple to white	late May to July	2–4 ft.
Mistflower (*Conoclinum coelestrinum*, formerly known as *Eupatorium coelestrinum*, and *Fleischmannia incarnata*, formerly known as *E. incarnata*)	perennial	blue, lavender, white	July to Sept.	1–3 ft.
Indian blanket (*Gaillardia pulchella*)	annual	yellow, orange, and red	June to Aug.	1–2 ft.
Blazingstar (*Liatris*)	perennial	purple to white	June to Sept.	1.5–5 ft.
Monarda (*Monarda fistulosa*)	perennial	pale lavender	June to July	1.5–3 ft.
Goldenrod (*Solidago*)	perennial	yellow	July to Oct.	1–5 ft.
Ironweed (*Vernonia*)	perennial	purple	July to Sept.	1–6 ft.

or nearby. For example, Hackberry Emperors (*Asterocampa celtis*) and American Snouts (*Libytheana carinenta*) are found near hackberries, and Black Swallowtails (*Papilio polyxenes*) occur near parsley, dill, fennel, and other related plants. Caterpillars of the stunning Gulf Fritillary (*Agraulis vanillae*) feed on the passionvine, which has equally impressive flowers. A number of butterflies and skippers feed on common weeds

Table 3.2 Easily cultivated nonnative species that are heavily used nectar sources

Name	Plant type	Flower color	Flowering season	Height
Garlic chives (*Allium tuberosum*)	perennial	white	July to Aug.	1.5–2.5 ft.
Basil (*Ocimum*)	annual	white	June to frost	1–2.5 ft.
Butterfly bush (*Buddleia*)	shrub	white, pink, red, purple, yellow	June to frost	up to 10 ft.
Globe amaranth (*Gomphrena*)	annual	white, pink, red purple, orange	June to frost	up to 2 ft.
Lantana (*Lantana*)	tender perennial	orange, yellow, purple, white	May to frost	up to 2 ft.
Pentas (*Pentas*)	tender perennial	white, pink, purple, red	May to frost	1–4 ft.
Salvia (*Salvia*)	annual or tender perennial	white, pink, red, purple, blue,	June to frost	1–4 ft.
Verbena (*Verbena*)	annual	white, pink, purple, red	June to frost	up to 2 ft.
Zinnia (*Zinnia*)	annual	all colors, except blue	June to frost	up to 5 ft.

such as lamb's-quarters, nettles, plantain, and thistles, and allowing a weedy area to remain in a corner of the yard or garden can provide a home to several more species.

If you are choosing plants to attract a particular butterfly species, remember to check first whether the butterfly occurs in your area. For example, planting pawpaw in central or western Oklahoma will probably not be successful in attracting Zebra Swallowtails (*Eurytides marcellus*) because it is found only in eastern Oklahoma.

To get the beautiful adults that we enjoy in our gardens, we need to accept some plant damage. The caterpillars of many butterflies feed on trees and shrubs, rarely reaching numbers high enough to be noticeable. The feeding damage can be pro-

FIG. 3.2. Black Swallowtail *(Papilio polyxenes)* larvae on parsley.

nounced, however, on a few herbaceous plants, especially those plants we grow to eat, such as parsley, dill, fennel, carrots, and cole crops (cabbage, broccoli, etc.). In such cases, we can plant more than we need and leave a portion of the crop for the caterpillars. Individual plants can be saved by moving caterpillars to other plants in the garden or by removing the butterfly eggs. Often predatory birds, mammals, insects, and spiders will seek out and catch the caterpillars before damage becomes severe. Providing a diverse, insecticide-free environment will encourage natural predators and greatly reduce the chance of extensive plant damage. Gardeners nevertheless need to decide how great a sacrifice is acceptable for the privilege of viewing the gorgeous creatures found in a butterfly-friendly garden.

Common native trees, shrubs, and herbaceous plants that serve as caterpillar host plants are listed in tables 3.3, 3.4, and 3.5, along with the butterfly species that favor them.

Plant Material Selection

Diversity is the key to attracting a wide range of butterfly species. Maximizing the number of butterflies in the garden requires that you provide a broad range of both nectar and caterpillar plants. The nectar plants should be selected so that at least one plant species is flowering at all times. Many annuals flower until frost and can provide the start of a successful garden. Annuals, however, must be planted each year after the danger of frost is past and may not start flowering until a few weeks after planting. Some annuals such as salvia are self-seeding and do not require replanting. Thus, spring-flowering perennials will be required to provide nectar sources in the spring. In general, once a perennial garden is established, it will require less work to maintain than a similar-sized garden filled with annuals. Most perennials, however, flower for only a few weeks,

Table 3.3 Common native trees that host one or more butterfly species

Name	Height[1]	Location[2]	Species Hosted	Comments
Pawpaw (*Asimina triloba*)	30 ft.	east	Zebra Swallowtail	occasionally produces fruit, which are edible
Hackberry (*Celtis*)	40 ft.	entire area	Hackberry Emperor Tawny Emperor American Snout Question Mark Mourning Cloak	hardy and durable
Redbud (*Cercis canadensis*)	20 ft.	east and central	Henry's Elfin	Oklahoma State Tree, beautiful spring flowers
Flowering Dogwood (*Cornus florida*)	40 ft.	east	Spring Azure Summer Azure	beautiful spring flowers and fall foliage and fruit; the fruit is a favorite of birds and squirrels
Red cedar (*Juniperus virginiana*)	40 ft.	entire area	Juniper Hairstreak	hardy and durable
Cottonwood (*Populus deltoides*)	75 ft.	entire area	Eastern Tiger Swallowtail Viceroy Red-spotted Purple Mourning Cloak	usually prefers a moist location; State Tree of Kansas

Table 3.3 continued

Name	Height[1]	Location[2]	Species Hosted	Comments
Black cherry (*Prunus serotina*)	50 ft.	east	Eastern Tiger Swallowtail Coral Hairstreak Red-spotted Purple	fruit can be used for preserves
Oak (*Quercus*)	up to 60 ft.	entire area	several hairstreaks and duskywings Red-spotted Purple	many species occur and they vary greatly in height
Black locust (*Robinia pseudoacacia*)	30 ft.	entire area	Silver-spotted Skipper	long clusters of white flowers in the spring
Willow (*Salix*)	up to 50 ft.	entire area	Viceroy Mourning Cloak Red-spotted Purple	usually prefers a moist location
Western soapberry (*Sapindus drumondii*)	25 ft.	entire area	Soapberry Hairstreak	hardy and durable, produces large attractive fruit
Sassafras (*Sassafras albidum*)	30 ft.	east	Spicebush Swallowtail	beautiful fall color
Elms (*Ulmus*)	60 ft.	east and central	Question Mark	several species occur

1. Mature height; individual plants may grow taller in favorable locations.
2. Portion of our area for which the species is best suited. Many plants can be grown outside the area noted if given a suitable location in the garden.

Table 3.4 Common native shrubs that host one or more butterfly species

Name	Height	Location[1]	Species hosted	Comments
New Jersey tea (*Ceanothus americanus*)	3 ft.	east, central	Summer Azure	clusters of small white flowers, leaves used by American Colonists
Spicebush (*Lindera benzoin*)	15 ft.	east	Spicebush and Eastern Tiger Swallowtails	prefers moist locations
Wild plum (*Prunus*)	8 ft.	entire area	Henry's Elfin Spring Azure Summer Azure Coral Hairstreak	edible fruit are a bonus
Blueberry (*Vaccinium*)	6 ft.	east	Henry's Elfin	edible fruit are a bonus with some species; one species, *V. arboreum*, is a small tree

1. Portion of our area for which the species is best suited. Many plants can be grown outside the area noted if given a suitable location in the garden.

and a sequence of different species will be required to obtain flowering from early spring to late fall. Long flowering periods for many perennial plants can be encouraged by deadheading—the practice of removing old flowers before seeds are produced.

To get the most out of your garden, use a variety of different types of plant materials: trees, shrubs, vines, and herbaceous plants. Trees and shrubs can be used as background plants, fences, or wind screens. Vines can be trained on walls or fences and will provide habitat for butterflies where none occurred before. Tall perennials can be mixed with shrubs or can be part of a flower garden mixed with annuals. For best viewing, place tall plants in the back of the garden or yard and progressively shorter plants in the front. Butterflies seem to be more attracted to masses of flowers rather than to isolated plantings.

Wherever possible, use native plants. Butterflies are already familiar with native plants as nectar sources and, in some cases, as caterpillar food. Many native plants also make excellent garden plants in that they are drought and heat tolerant. Some of our most spectacular native wildflowers work well in a home garden.

Location

Butterflies are ectothermic animals and consequently need warm temperatures or the heat of sunlight to fly. A sunny location will allow butterflies to bask in the sunlight and warm up during cool weather from fall to spring and on cool mornings. A few butterflies are adapted to shady woodland conditions, but most prefer the bright sunshine of fields and woodland openings. In addition, the majority of the favorite plants for nectar or for caterpillar food require a mostly sunny location.

Butterflies also prefer a location sheltered from the wind. A few butterflies can be found at exposed locations even on the

Table 3.5 Common native herbaceous plants that host one or more butterfly species

Name	Height/length	Location[1]	Species hosted	Comments
Pipevines (*Aristolochia*)	25 ft.	far east	Pipevine Swallowtail	vine, unusually shaped flowers in summer
Perennial asters (*Aster*)	1–4 ft.	entire area	Pearl Crescent Silvery Checkerspot	white, pink, purple flowers from July to Oct.
Milkweed (*Asclepias*)	1–2.5 ft.	entire area	Monarch Queen	orange, yellow, pink flowers from May to Sept., depending on species
Wild indigo (*Baptisia*)	2–3 ft.	entire area	Hoary Edge Wild Indigo Duskywing	blue, white, or yellow flowers in the spring
Partridge pea (*Chamaecrista fasciculata*, formerly known as *Cassia fasciculata*)	1–3 ft.	entire area	Cloudless Sulphur Little Yellow Sleepy Orange	yellow flowers in summer

Table 3.5 (continued)

Name	Height/length	Location[1]	Species hosted	Comments
Grasses (many species)	1–8 ft.	entire area	many skippers and satyrs	many ornamental grasses are available
Passionvine (*Passiflora*)	20 ft.	east	Gulf and Variegated Fritillaries	vine, intricate white, blue, or pale yellow flowers from July to frost
Violets (*Viola*)	4–12 in.	entire area	Variegated, Diana, Great Spangled, and Regal Fritillaries	white, blue, yellow flowers in spring; many species occur
Yucca (*Yucca*)	5 ft.	entire area	Yucca Giant-Skipper	large clusters of white flowers in early summer

1. Portion of our area for which the species is best suited. Many plants can be grown outside the area noted if given a suitable location in the garden.

windiest days, but they will be easier to watch, photograph, and enjoy in a sheltered garden. The wind protection can be provided by trees, shrubs, or tall herbaceous plants or by structures such as fences and buildings.

Minimizing Insecticide Use

Avoid using insecticides. Some products are specifically designed to kill butterfly, skipper, and moth caterpillars, as will be indicated on the container label. Other pesticides are general and designed to kill a broad spectrum of insects. Read pesticide labels and look for the names of pest insects that are moths, butterflies, or skippers and for the word *caterpillar*.

If you must use an insecticide as a last resort, apply it carefully with a small hand-operated spray bottle so that the spray can be directed only at the plants with the target pest. Avoid applying pesticide on windy days when it can drift and kill nontarget insects. Use the least toxic pesticide available, such as an insecticidal soap, and note that even if a product is labeled "natural" or "organic," it may kill butterflies. Always opt on the side of caution, as the use of pesticides not only harms butterflies and beneficial insects such as solitary wasps and bees but can also have other adverse effects on the environment.

Miscellaneous Elements

A number of additional items can round out the well-planned butterfly garden. A moist area of soil or sand, alone or next to a water garden, can provide a place for butterflies to puddle, the process of imbibing salts and water (fig. 3.3). Dripping hoses or manufactured drippers can provide moist areas from splashing water. A favorite puddling spot may attract dozens of individuals of several species. Puddling butterflies usually are males, but careful observation may yield females.

FIG. 3.3. Sulphurs puddling.

The presence of leaf litter may provide food for one of the common and beautiful butterflies of the southern plains, the Red-banded Hairstreak (*Calycopis cecrops*). This species prefers fallen sumac or oak leaves but may be found in the dead leaves of other plants. In addition some species, such as Hackberry Emperor, Tawny Emperor (*Asterocampa clyton*), and the strikingly beautiful Great Purple Hairstreak (*Atlides halesus*), overwinter as larvae or pupae in leaf litter. By not raking leaves in the fall below the host plant, you will help preserve future generations of these overwintering butterfly species. They will reward you by frequenting your garden the following summer.

Shelter can also be provided for butterflies that overwinter as adults, such as Mourning Cloak (*Nymphalis antiopa*), Question Mark, and Eastern Comma (*Polygonia comma*). These species may use a permanent wood pile of generously spaced logs, stacked with each level running in the opposite direction to the level below it and placed in an unkempt area of your property. Commercial butterfly hibernation boxes appear to attract only wasps and are ignored by the butterflies, which prefer to winter behind loose tree bark or, if you are lucky, in the above-mentioned wood pile.

The adults of several common species such as Red Admirals (*Vanessa atalanta*), Question Marks, Eastern Commas, Goatweed Leafwings (*Anaea andria*), Hackberry Emperors, Tawny Emperors, and Red-spotted Purples (*Limenitis arthemis astyanax*) typically do not nectar and are attracted to rotting fruits, such as bananas, apples, watermelons, or cantaloupes. The fruit can be placed in the compost pile or on a butterfly feeder. A butterfly feeder can be any flat surface in a sunny location. The feeder works best when placed one to four feet above the ground but may need to be moved higher to prevent foraging raccoons, squirrels, opossums, and skunks from taking the fruit (fig. 3.4).

FIG. 3.4. Fruit offered on a butterfly feeder can attract species that do not feed on nectar.

4

Butterfly Hotspots

Butterflies can be found almost anywhere in the southern plains, with interesting species turning up in the most unlikely places. In populated areas, check local gardens and natural areas. Even a weedy city lot or unused railroad line with numerous flowers may provide a nice selection of butterfly species. Wild areas with a broad range of habitats including woods, scrub, fields, ponds, and streams will generally provide the greatest number of butterfly species. Some locations are well known as places to find greater than normal numbers and species of butterflies. In some of these areas, particularly Nature Conservancy preserves, collecting of butterflies and other organisms is not permitted; be sure to bring close-focusing binoculars for maximum enjoyment of the butterflies.

Central Kansas

Botanica, Wichita. This beautiful garden features both a 2,800-square-foot indoor butterfly hoop house and an outdoor butterfly garden. The butterfly house is open from June through October. The gardens host a good selection of regularly occurring species. Botanica is located in Sim Park at Murdock and Amidon, and its hours are 9:00 A.M. to 5:00 P.M. Monday through Saturday, 1:00 to 5:00 P.M. on Sunday, and open until 8:00 P.M. on Tuesday evenings.

Chisholm Creek Park. With 240 acres, Chisholm Creek Park includes a broad range of habitats from native and restored prairie to scrub, wetland, and woods. The diversity of habitats provides a great selection of central Kansas butterflies. The park is open dawn to dusk year-round and the nature center is open 9:00 A.M. to 5:00 P.M. Monday through Saturday, year-round except for holidays. The park has entrances at 6232 E. 29th Street North and 3238 N. Oliver and is located within the Wichita City limits.

Chase State Fishing Lake and Tallgrass Prairie National Preserve. These two areas highlight remnants of the magnificent tallgrass prairie habitat in the Flint Hills. Chase State Fishing Lake is surrounded by classic tallgrass prairie, with riparian habitat around the lake and streams. The 11,000-acre Tallgrass Prairie National Preserve is well named and has a fine three-story visitor center that is part of the National Park System. Both locations host the very local and spectacular Regal Fritillary (*Speyeria idalia*) as well as a broad array of other prairie species. Look for scrub and woodland species in the riparian areas. Chase State Fishing Lake is located approximately two miles west of Cottonwood Falls off of Lake Road and includes a camping area. Tallgrass Prairie Preserve is on highway 177 just north of highway 56. The preserve headquarters and nature trail are open daily 9:00 A.M. to 4:00 P.M., except for some holidays.

Gypsum Hills. West of Medicine Lodge is an area known as the Gypsum Hills or the Red Hills, stretching from Kansas through Oklahoma to North Texas. This scenic area has rolling hills and rocky slopes with exposed, bright red clay. Some of the small plateaus are topped with a thick layer of white gypsum.

The vegetation is a mixed-grass prairie with sectors of cedar. The whole area can be spectacular with wildflowers in the spring, especially in May, and hosts a number of western butterfly species. The Gypsum Hills can be reached by driving northwest from Medicine Lodge to Sun City and taking one of several roads south to Highway 160. Watch weather conditions, as the roads may be impassable in wet weather.

McPherson State Fishing Lake and Maxwell Wildlife Refuge. These are two more locations to see tallgrass prairie and its associated species, such as the Regal Fritillary, which is especially prevalent in late June. McPherson Lake has prairie on its eastern side and woods on its south and west sides. McPherson State Fishing Lake is located near Canton at the intersection of Highways 56 and 86. The 2,234-acre Maxwell Wildlife Refuge is immediately adjacent to the McPherson State Fishing Lake, six miles north of Canton off McPherson County Road 304, and hosts a herd of bison and elk.

Eastern Oklahoma

Tallgrass Prairie Preserve. One of the largest remaining tallgrass prairies in the country, this preserve hosts an annual North American Butterfly Association (NABA) butterfly count (see table 4.1). Trails have been established to provide access to the great selection of prairie butterflies that can be found here, including the rare Byssus Skipper (*Problema byssus*) and Gray Copper (*Lycaena dione*). The magnificent Regal Fritillary, designated an endangered species in Oklahoma, has also been spotted here on rare occasions. The Tallgrass Prairie Preserve is administered by the Nature Conservancy and is located approximately 15 minutes north of Pawhuska. A picnic area and gift shop are located near the Tallgrass Prairie National Preserve headquarters.

Table 4.1. Butterflies and skippers of the Tallgrass
Prairie Preserve, Pawhuska, Oklahoma

Species	Status
Pipevine Swallowtail *Battus philenor*	Uncommon
Zebra Swallowtail *Eurytides marcellus*	Vagrant
Black Swallowtail *Papilio polyxenes*	Common
Giant Swallowtail *Papilio cresphontes*	Rare
Eastern Tiger Swallowtail *Papilio glaucus*	Common
Spicebush Swallowtail *Papilio troilus*	Rare
Checkered White *Pontia protodice*	Uncommon
Cabbage White *Pieris rapae*	Rare
Olympia Marble *Euchloe olympia*	Rare
Falcate Orangetip *Anthocharis midea*	Rare
Clouded Sulphur *Colias philodice*	Rare
Orange Sulphur *Colias eurytheme*	Common
Southern Dogface *Colias cesonia*	Rare
Cloudless Sulphur *Phoebis sennae*	Common
Little Yellow *Eurema lisa*	Common
Sleepy Orange *Eurema nicippe*	Common
Dainty Sulphur *Nathalis iole*	Common
Harvester *Feniseca tarquinius*	Rare
Gray Copper *Lycaena dione*	Rare
Edwards' Hairstreak *Satyrium edwardsii*	Rare
Banded Hairstreak *Satyrium calanus*	Rare
Juniper Hairstreak *Callophrys gryneus*	Rare
Gray Hairstreak *Strymon melinus*	Common
Red-banded Hairstreak *Calycopis cecrops*	Uncommon
Marine Blue *Leptotes marina*	Rare
Reakirt's Blue *Hemiargus isola*	Uncommon
Eastern Tailed-Blue *Everes comyntas*	Abundant
Spring Azure *Celastrina ladon*	Uncommon
Summer Azure *Celastrina neglecta*	Uncommon
American Snout *Libytheana carinenta*	Uncommon
Gulf Fritillary *Agraulis vanillae*	Uncommon
Variegated Fritillary *Euptoieta claudia*	Common
Regal Fritillary *Speyeria idalia*	Rare

Table 4.1 (continued)

Species	Status
Gorgone Checkerspot *Chlosyne gorgone*	Rare
Silvery Checkerspot *Chlosyne nycteis*	Rare
Phaon Cresent *Phyciodes phaon*	Rare
Pearl Crescent *Phyciodes tharos*	Abundant
Question Mark *Polygonia interrogationis*	Common
Mourning Cloak *Nymphalis antiopa*	Rare
American Lady *Vanessa virginiensis*	Common
Painted Lady *Vanessa cardui*	Uncommon
Red Admiral *Vanessa atalanta*	Common
Common Buckeye *Junonia coenia*	Common
Red-spotted Purple *Limenitis arthemis astyanax*	Rare
Viceroy *Limenitis archippus*	Rare
Goatweed Leafwing *Anaea andria*	Common
Hackberry Emperor *Asterocampa celtis*	Uncommon
Tawny Emperor *Asterocampa clyton*	Rare
Northern Pearly-eye *Enodia anthedon*	Uncommon
Gemmed Satyr *Cyllopsis gemma*	Uncommon
Little Wood-Satyr *Megisto cymela*	Common
Common Wood-Nymph *Cercyonis pegala*	Common
Monarch *Danaus plexippus*	Common
Silver-spotted Skipper *Epargyreus clarus*	Common
Hoary Edge *Achalarus lyciades*	Rare
Southern Cloudywing *Thorybes bathyllus*	Common
Northern Cloudywing *Thorybes pylades*	Common
Confused Cloudywing *Thorybes confusis*	Rare
Hayhurst's Scallopwing *Staphylus hayhurstii*	Rare
Juvenal's Duskywing *Erynnis juvenalis*	Common
Horace's Duskywing *Erynnis horatius*	Common
Funereal Duskywing *Erynnis funeralis*	Rare
Wild Indigo Duskywing *Erynnis baptisiae*	Rare
Common Checkered-Skipper *Pyrgus communis*	Common
Common Sootywing *Pholisora catullus*	Rare
Least Skipper *Ancyloxypha numitor*	Uncommon
Orange Skipperling *Copaeodes aurantiacus*	Rare
Fiery Skipper *Hylephila phyleus*	Common

Table 4.1 (continued)

Species	Status
Tawny-edged Skipper *Polites themistocles*	Common
Crossline Skipper *Polites origenes*	Uncommon
Sachem *Atalopedes campestris*	Common
Arogos Skipper *Atrytone arogos*	Rare
Delaware Skipper *Anatrytone logan*	Rare
Byssus Skipper *Problema byssus*	Rare
Zabulon Skipper *Poanes zabulon*	Uncommon
Dun Skipper *Euphyes vestris metacomet*	Uncommon
Dusted Skipper *Atrytonopsis hianna*	Rare
Common Roadside-Skipper *Amblyscirtes vialis*	Rare
Eufala Skipper *Lerodea eufala*	Rare
Ocola Skipper *Panoquina ocola*	Vagrant

Abundant = Many individuals of this species be found every visit during normal flight period.

Common = One or more individuals of this species can be found every visit during normal flight period.

Uncommon = One or more individuals of this species can be found on some visits during normal flight period.

Rare = Generally recorded once a year or less frequently.

Vagrant = Has been recorded but is unlikely to be found again.

Talimena Drive and Adjacent Parks. One of the most beautiful areas of southeast Oklahoma, this area also hosts a wide variety of butterflies. Six species of swallowtails can be found in one day: Pipevine (*Battus philenor*), Black (*Papilio polyxenes*), Giant (*P. cresphontes*), Eastern Tiger (*P. glaucus*), Spicebush (*P. troilus*) and Zebra (*Eurytides marcellus*). Numerous satyrs and skippers, including the Sleepy Duskywing (*Erynnis brizo*), can also be found in the area. The Talimena Drive extends from Talihina, Oklahoma, to Mena, Arkansas, along Highway 1.

Central Oklahoma

Oklahoma Botanical Garden and Arboretum (OBGA). A wide range of plants and habitats can be found on the 80-acre

OBGA. Of special interest are the studio gardens for the television show *Oklahoma Gardening,* which sometimes includes a butterfly garden. Close to 50 species have been found at OBGA in a single August day; up to 65 species are typically found over the course of a year (table 4.2). A number of locally unusual or rare species have occurred, including the Long-tailed Skipper (*Urbanus proteus*), Mexican Yellow (*Eurema mexicana*), and Texan Crescent (*Phyciodes texana*). OBGA regularly hosts Gulf Fritillaries (*Agraulis vanillae*), Giant Swallowtails, Gorgone and Silvery Checkerspots (*Chlosyne gorgone, C. nycteis*), Juniper Hairstreaks (*Callophrys gryneus*), and Nysa and Bell's Roadside-Skippers (*Amblyscirtes nysa, A. belli*). OBGA is located on the west side of Stillwater on Virginia Street.

Table 4.2. Butterflies and skippers of the Oklahoma Botanical Garden and Arboretum, Stillwater, Oklahoma

Species	Status
Pipevine Swallowtail *Battus philenor*	Uncommon
Black Swallowtail *Papilio polyxenes*	Common
Giant Swallowtail *Papilio cresphontes*	Rare
Eastern Tiger Swallowtail *Papilio glaucus*	Common
Checkered White *Pontia protodice*	Common
Cabbage White *Pieris rapae*	Common
Clouded Sulphur *Colias philodice*	Rare
Orange Sulphur *Colias eurytheme*	Common
Cloudless Sulphur *Phoebis sennae*	Common
Mexican Yellow *Eurema mexicana*	Rare
Little Yellow *Eurema lisa*	Uncommon
Sleepy Orange *Eurema nicippe*	Rare
Dainty Sulphur *Nathalis iole*	Abundant
Oak Hairstreak *Satyrium favonius*	Rare
Juniper Hairstreak *Callophrys gryneus*	Rare
Gray Hairstreak *Strymon melinus*	Common

Table 4.2 (continued)

Species	Status
Red-banded Hairstreak *Calycopis cecrops*	Common
Western Pygmy-Blue *Brephidium exile*	Rare
Marine Blue *Leptotes marina*	Rare
Reakirt's Blue *Hemiargus isola*	Uncommon
Eastern Tailed-Blue *Everes comyntas*	Common
Spring Azure *Celastrina ladon*	Rare
Summer Azure *Celastrina neglecta*	Rare
American Snout *Libytheana carinenta*	Common
Gulf Fritillary *Agraulis vanillae*	Common
Variegated Fritillary *Euptoieta claudia*	Common
Gorgone Checkerspot *Chlosyne gorgone*	Common
Silvery Checkerspot *Chlosyne nycteis*	Uncommon
Texan Crescent *Phyciodes texana*	Rare
Pearl Crescent *Phyciodes tharos*	Common
Question Mark *Polygonia interrogationis*	Common
American Lady *Vanessa virginiensis*	Common
Painted Lady *Vanessa cardui*	Common
Red Admiral *Vanessa atalanta*	Uncommon
Common Buckeye *Junonia coenia*	Common
Red-spotted Purple *Limenitis arthemis astyanax*	Uncommon
Viceroy *Limenitis archippus*	Uncommon
Goatweed Leafwing *Anaea andria*	Uncommon
Hackberry Emperor *Asterocampa celtis*	Common
Tawny Emperor *Asterocampa clyton*	Rare
Little Wood-Satyr *Megisto cymela*	Rare
Common Wood-Nymph *Cercyonis pegala*	Uncommon
Monarch *Danaus plexippus*	Common
Silver-spotted Skipper *Epargyreus clarus*	Common
Long-tailed Skipper *Urbanus proteus*	Vagrant
Hoary Edge *Achalarus lyciades*	Rare
Southern Cloudywing *Thorybes bathyllus*	Common
Northern Cloudywing *Thorybes pylades*	Rare
Hayhurst's Scallopwing *Staphylus hayhurstii*	Uncommon
Juvenal's Duskywing *Erynnis juvenalis*	Uncommon

Table 4.2 (continued)

Species	Status
Horace's Duskywing *Erynnis horatius*	Uncommon
Funereal Duskywing *Erynnis funeralis*	Rare
Wild Indigo Duskywing *Erynnis baptisiae*	Rare
Common Checkered-Skipper *Pyrgus communis*	Common
Common Sootywing *Pholisora catullus*	Uncommon
Clouded Skipper *Lerema accius*	Uncommon
Least Skipper *Ancyloxypha numitor*	Vagrant
Fiery Skipper *Hylephila phyleus*	Common
Tawny-edged Skipper *Polites themistocles*	Common
Crossline Skipper *Polites origenes*	Uncommon
Southern Broken-Dash *Wallengrenia otho*	Uncommon
Sachem *Atalopedes campestris*	Abundant
Delaware Skipper *Anatrytone logan*	Rare
Zabulon Skipper *Poanes zabulon*	Uncommon
Dion Skipper *Euphyes dion*	Vagrant
Dun Skipper *Euphyes vestris metacomet*	Uncommon
Nysa Roadside-Skipper *Amblyscirtes nysa*	Uncommon
Common Roadside-Skipper *Amblyscirtes vialis*	Common
Bell's Roadside-Skipper *Amblyscirtes belli*	Uncommon
Eufala Skipper *Lerodea eufala*	Uncommon
Ocola Skipper *Panoquina ocola*	Vagrant

Abundant = Many individuals of this species be found every visit during normal flight
   period.
Common = One or more individuals of this species can be found every visit during
   normal flight period.
Uncommon = One or more individuals of this species can be found on some visits
   during normal flight period.
Rare = Generally recorded once a year or less frequently.
Vagrant = Has been recorded but is unlikely to be found again.

Oklahoma City Zoo Butterfly Garden. This beautiful, medium-sized garden hosts a large number of species. Giant, Black, and Tiger Swallowtails are common. Several unusual species found in the gardens include Zebra Heliconian (*Heliconius charithonia*), Queen (*Danaus gilippus*), and Southern

Dogface (*Colias cesonia*). A large number of more common central Oklahoma species can also be seen here.

Pontotoc Ridge Preserve. One of the prime areas for butterflying in Oklahoma is the Nature Conservancy's 2,900-acre Pontotoc Ridge Preserve located approximately 15 miles south of Ada in south-central Oklahoma. Along with myriads of wildflowers, it is possible to see more than 40 butterfly species in a day (table 4.3). This preserve hosts an annual NABA butterfly count and is a paradise for skipper enthusiasts, with such attractions as the Green Skipper (*Hesperia viridis*), Dotted Skipper (*H. attalus*), and Arogos Skipper (*Atrytone arogos*). The large number of Arogos Skippers found here is indicative of undisturbed habitat. Trails have been established throughout the preserve and there is a picnic area. Before visiting this highly recommended hotspot, however, you must obtain permission from the Nature Conservancy's onsite office (580-777-2224).

Table 4.3. Butterflies and skippers of the Pontotoc Ridge Preserve, Ada, Oklahoma

Species	Status
Pipevine Swallowtail *Battus philenor*	Common
Black Swallowtail *Papilio polyxenes*	Common
Giant Swallowtail *Papilio cresphontes*	Common
Eastern Tiger Swallowtail *Papilio glaucus*	Common
Spicebush Swallowtail *Papilio troilus*	Rare
Checkered White *Pontia protodice*	Uncommon
Falcate Orangetip *Anthocharis midea*	Rare
Clouded Sulphur *Colias philodice*	Uncommon
Orange Sulphur *Colias eurytheme*	Common
Southern Dogface *Colias cesonia*	Rare
Cloudless Sulphur *Phoebis sennae*	Common
Mexican Yellow *Eurema mexicana*	Uncommon
Little Yellow *Eurema lisa*	Abundant
Sleepy Orange *Eurema nicippe*	Common

Table 4.3 (continued)

Species	Status
Dainty Sulphur *Nathalis iole*	Abundant
Great Purple Hairstreak *Atlides halesus*	Rare
Soapberry Hairstreak *Phaeostrymon alcestis*	Rare
Coral Hairstreak *Satyrium titus*	Common
Edwards' Hairstreak *Satyrium edwardsii*	Rare
Banded Hairstreak *Satyrium calanus*	Rare
Gray Hairstreak *Strymon melinus*	Common
Red-banded Hairstreak *Calycopis cecrops*	Uncommon
Marine Blue *Leptotes marina*	Rare
Reakirt's Blue *Hemiargus isola*	Common
Eastern Tailed-Blue *Everes comyntas*	Abundant
Spring Azure *Celastrina ladon*	Common
Summer Azure *Celastrina neglecta*	Common
American Snout *Libytheana carinenta*	Uncommon
Gulf Fritillary *Agraulis vanillae*	Uncommon
Variegated Fritillary *Euptoieta claudia*	Abundant
Gorgone Checkerspot *Chlosyne gorgone*	Uncommon
Silvery Checkerspot *Chlosyne nycteis*	Uncommon
Pearl Crescent *Phyciodes tharos*	Abundant
Question Mark *Polygonia interrogationis*	Common
Eastern Comma *Polygonia comma*	Rare
Mourning Cloak *Nymphalis antiopa*	Rare
American Lady *Vanessa virginiensis*	Common
Painted Lady *Vanessa cardui*	Common
Red Admiral *Vanessa atalanta*	Common
Common Buckeye *Junonia coenia*	Common
Red-spotted Purple *Limenitis arthemis astyanax*	Uncommon
Viceroy *Limenitis archippus*	Uncommon
Goatweed Leafwing *Anaea andria*	Common
Hackberry Emperor *Asterocampa celtis*	Common
Tawny Emperor *Asterocampa clyton*	Uncommon
Northern Pearly-eye *Enodia anthedon*	Common
Gemmed Satyr *Cyllopsis gemma*	Uncommon
Carolina Satyr *Hermeuptychia sosybius*	Common

Table 4.3 (continued)

Species	Status
Little Wood-Satyr *Megisto cymela*	Common
Common Wood-Nymph *Cercyonis pegala*	Common
Monarch *Danaus plexippus*	Common
Queen *Danaus gilippus*	Rare
Silver-spotted Skipper *Epargyreus clarus*	Common
Long-tailed Skipper *Urbanus proteus*	Vagrant
Hoary Edge *Achalarus lyciades*	Rare
Southern Cloudywing *Thorybes bathyllus*	Common
Northern Cloudywing *Thorybes pylades*	Common
Confused Cloudywing *Thorybes confusis*	Rare
Hayhurst's Scallopwing *Staphylus hayhurstii*	Rare
Juvenal's Duskywing *Erynnis juvenalis*	Common
Horace's Duskywing *Erynnis horatius*	Common
Mottled Duskywing *Erynnis martialis*	Rare
Funereal Duskywing *Erynnis funeralis*	Rare
Wild Indigo Duskywing *Erynnis baptisiae*	Uncommon
Common Checkered-Skipper *Pyrgus communis*	Common
Common Sootywing *Pholisora catullus*	Rare
Swarthy Skipper *Nastra lherminier*	Rare
Clouded Skipper *Lerema accius*	Rare
Least Skipper *Ancyloxypha numitor*	Rare
Orange Skipperling *Copaeodes aurantiacus*	Rare
Fiery Skipper *Hylephila phyleus*	Common
Green Skipper *Hesperia viridis*	Rare
Dotted Skipper *Hesperia attalus*	Rare
Tawny-edged Skipper *Polites themistocles*	Common
Crossline Skipper *Polites origenes*	Common
Southern Boken-Dash *Wallengrenia otho*	Uncommon
Northern Boken-Dash *Wallengrenia egeremet*	Rare
Sachem *Atalopedes campestris*	Abundant
Arogos Skipper *Atrytone arogos*	Common
Delaware Skipper *Anatrytone logan*	Rare
Zabulon Skipper *Poanes zabulon*	Uncommon
Dun Skipper *Euphyes vestris metacomet*	Common
Dusted Skipper *Atrytonopsis hianna*	Rare
Eufala Skipper *Lerodea eufala*	Uncommon

Table 4.3 (continued)

Species	Status

Abundant = Many individuals of this species be found every visit during normal flight period.

Common = One or more individuals of this species can be found every visit during normal flight period.

Uncommon = One or more individuals of this species can be found on some visits during normal flight period.

Rare = Generally recorded once a year or less frequently.

Vagrant = Has been recorded but is unlikely to be found again.

Western Oklahoma

Wichita Mountains National Wildlife Refuge. The beautiful Wichita Mountains National Wildlife Refuge has hosted an annual NABA butterfly count for several years (table 4.4). Habitats include broad expanses of shortgrass prairie, oak-covered hillsides, and rocky ravines. The rare and local Red Satyr (*Megisto rubricata*) and the striking California Sister (*Adepha bredowii*) have been seen in the area. The Wichita Mountains National Wildlife Refuge is located west of Lawton.

Table 4.4. Butterflies and skippers of the Wichita Mountains National Wildlife Refuge, Lawton, Oklahoma

Species	Status
Black Swallowtail *Papillo polyxenes*	Common
Giant Swallowtail *Papilio cresphontes*	Uncommon
Eastern Tiger Swallowtail *Papilio glaucus*	Rare
Checkered White *Pontia protodice*	Uncommon
Cabbage White *Pieris rapae*	Common
Clouded Sulphur *Colias philodice*	Uncommon
Orange Sulphur *Colias eurytheme*	Common
Cloudless Sulphur *Phoebis sennae*	Uncommon
Southern Dogface *Colias cesonia*	Rare

Table 4.4 (continued)

Species	Status
Sleepy Orange *Eurema nicippe*	Common
Dainty Sulphur *Nathalis iole*	Abundant
Gray Hairstreak *Strymon melinus*	Rare
Reakirt's Blue *Hemiargus isola*	Uncommon
Eastern Tailed-Blue *Everes comyntas*	Common
Silvery Blue *Glaucopsyche lygdamus*	Rare
Variegated Fritillary *Euptoieta claudia*	Common
Pearl Crescent *Phyciodes tharos*	Common
Question Mark *Polygonia interrogationis*	Uncommon
Painted Lady *Vanessa cardui*	Common
Red Admiral *Vanessa atalanta*	Common
Common Buckeye *Junonia coenia*	Common
Goatweed Leafwing *Anaea andria*	Uncommon
Hackberry Emperor *Asterocampa celtis*	Common
Tawny Emperor *Asterocampa clyton*	Rare
Northern Pearly-eye *Enodia anthedon*	Rare
Gemmed Satyr *Cyllopsis gemma*	Rare
Little Wood-Satyr *Megisto cymela*	Common
Red Satyr *Megisto rubricata*	Uncommon
Common Wood-Nymph *Cercyonis pegala*	Common
Monarch *Danaus plexippus*	Common
Queen *Danaus gilippus*	Rare
Northern Cloudywing *Thorybes pylades*	Uncommon
Common Checkered-Skipper *Pyrgus communis*	Common
Common Sootywing *Pholisora catullus*	Uncommon
Orange Skipperling *Copaeodes aurantiacus*	Uncommon
Sachem *Atalopedes campestris*	Uncommon

Abundant = Many individuals of this species be found every visit during normal flight period.

Common = One or more individuals of this species can be found every visit during normal flight period.

Uncommon = One or more individuals of this species can be found on some visits during normal flight period.

Rare = Generally recorded once a year or less frequently.

Vagrant = Has been recorded but is unlikely to be found again.

Red River and Nearby Countryside. When butterfly season has come to a close in most parts of Oklahoma, it is time to head to the Red River and surrounding areas. In late summer and fall, look for large numbers of Queens, Texan Crescents, Western Pygmy-Blues (*Brephidium exilis*), Sleepy Oranges (*Eurema nicippe*), and Funereal Duskywings (*Erynnis funeralis*) along Oklahoma's southern border. Prime locations are south of the town of El Dorado.

Black Mesa and Nearby Countryside. To find western butterflies in Oklahoma, one must travel to the panhandle. In particular, the northwest corner of Cimarron County is both beautiful and frequently full of butterflies. Select canyons within the area are host to Two-tailed Swallowtails (*Papilio multicaudata*), Viereck's Skipper (*Atrytonopsis vierecki*), and Bronze Roadside-Skippers (*Amblyscirtes aenus*). More widely distributed are the Southern Dogface, Acmon Blue (*Plebejus acmon*), Melissa Blue (*Lycaeides melissa*), and Painted Crescents (*Phyciodes picta*). The roads and mesas around Kenton and Lake Etling State Park are prime locations to explore. Numerous rare species have occurred in the area over the years—who knows what discoveries await the next butterflier?

North-Central Texas

Caddo–Lyndon B. Johnson National Grasslands. Located just 45 minutes northwest of Fort Worth, the L.B.J. National Grasslands encompasses over 20,000 acres of grass and other wild lands. One prime location is the Black Creek Lake Recreation Area, seven miles north of Decatur. The L.B.J. Grasslands are especially good in March and April when Olympia Marbles (*Euchloe olympia*), Falcate Orangetips (*Anthocharis midea*), and Yucca Giant-Skippers (*Megathymus yuccae*) can be seen. A wide range of species can be found during the warm months. The Grasslands has hiking trails, picnicking areas, camping, and boating.

Fort Worth Botanical Garden. Known for attracting interesting southern migrants, this 109-acre botanical garden has established gardens, wooded areas, and open fields. Notable species seen have included Zebra Heliconians and Julia Heliconians (*Dryas iulia*). A wide variety of species are possible (table 4.5). The Fort Worth Botanical Garden is located in Trinity Park about three miles west from downtown Fort Worth and has two gates, one on University Avenue and one on Harley. The visitor center is open seven days a week.

Table 4.5. Butterflies and skippers of Tarrant County, Texas, including the Fort Worth Nature Center and Fort Worth Botanical Garden

Species	Status
Pipevine Swallowtail *Battus philenor*	Common
Black Swallowtail *Papilio polyxenes*	Abundant
Giant Swallowtail *Papilio cresphontes*	Abundant
Eastern Tiger Swallowtail *Papilio glaucus*	Abundant
Checkered White *Pontia protodice*	Uncommon
Cabbage White *Pieris rapae*	Abundant
Falcate Orangetip *Anthocharis midea*	Rare
Orange Sulphur *Colias eurytheme*	Abundant
Southern Dogface *Colias cesonia*	Common
Cloudless Sulphur *Phoebis sennae*	Abundant
Mexican Yellow *Eurema mexicana*	Rare
Little Yellow *Eurema lisa*	Abundant
Sleepy Orange *Eurema nicippe*	Abundant
Dainty Sulphur *Nathalis iole*	Abundant
Harvester *Feniseca tarquinus*	Rare
Great Purple Hairstreak *Atlides halesus*	Common
Soapberry Hairstreak *Phaeostrymon alcestis*	Common
Coral Hairstreak *Satyrium titus*	Rare
Banded Hairstreak *Satyrium calanus*	Common
Oak Hairstreak *Satyrium favonius*	Common

Table 4.5 (continued)

Species	Status
Henry's Elfin *Callophrys henrici*	Common
Juniper Hairstreak *Callophrys gryneus*	Uncommon
White M Hairstreak *Parrhasius m-album*	Uncommon
Gray Hairstreak *Strymon melinus*	Abundant
Red-banded Hairstreak *Calycopis cecrops*	Uncommon
Dusky-blue Groundstreak *Calycopis isobeon*	Uncommon
Western Pygmy-Blue *Brephidium exile*	Rare
Marine Blue *Leptotes marina*	Uncommon
Ceraunus Blue *Hemiargus ceraunus*	Uncommon
Reakirt's Blue *Hemiargus isola*	Abundant
Eastern Tailed-Blue *Everes comyntas*	Common
Spring Azure *Celastrina ladon*	Rare
Summer Azure *Celastrina neglecta*	Rare
American Snout *Libytheana carinenta*	Common
Gulf Fritillary *Agraulis vanillae*	Abundant
Julia Heliconian *Dryas iulia*	Rare
Zebra Heliconian *Heliconius charithonia*	Rare
Variegated Fritillary *Euptoieta claudia*	Abundant
Bordered Patch *Chlosyne lacinia*	Uncommon
Gorgone Checkerspot *Chlosyne gorgone*	Uncommon
Silvery Checkerspot *Chlosyne nycteis*	Uncommon
Texas Crescent *Phyciodes texana*	Common
Phaon Crescent *Phyciodes phaon*	Abundant
Pearl Crescent *Phyciodes tharos*	Abundant
Question Mark *Polygonia interrogationis*	Common
Mourning Cloak *Nymphalis antiopa*	Rare
American Lady *Vanessa virginiensis*	Abundant
Painted Lady *Vanessa cardui*	Common
Red Admiral *Vanessa atalanta*	Common
Common Buckeye *Junonia coenia*	Abundant
Red-spotted Purple *Limenitis arthemis astyanax*	Uncommon
Viceroy *Limenitis archippus*	Uncommon
California Sister *Adelpha bredowii*	Rare
Common Mestra *Mestra amymone*	Rare
Goatweed Leafwing *Anaea andria*	Uncommon

Table 4.5 (continued)

Species	Status
Hackberry Emperor *Asterocampa celtis*	Abundant
Tawny Emperor *Asterocampa clyton*	Common
Little Wood-Satyr *Megisto cymela*	Common
Red Satyr *Megisto rubricata*	Uncommon
Common Wood-Nymph *Cercyonis pegala*	Abundant
Monarch *Danaus plexippus*	Common
Queen *Danaus gilippus*	Abundant
Silver-spotted Skipper *Epargyreus clarus*	Common
Long-tailed Skipper *Urbanus proteus*	Rare
Hoary Edge *Achalarus lyciades*	Uncommon
Southern Cloudywing *Thorybes bathyllus*	Uncommon
Northern Cloudywing *Thorybes pylades*	Common
Confused Cloudywing *Thorybes confusis*	Uncommon
Outis Skipper *Cogia outis*	Common
Hayhurst's Scallopwing *Staphylus hayhurstii*	Common
Sickle-winged Skipper *Achlyodes thraso*	Rare
Sleepy Duskywing *Erynnis brizo*	Uncommon
Juvenal's Duskywing *Erynnis juvenalis*	Common
Horace's Duskywing *Erynnis horatius*	Common
Zarucco Duskywing *Erynnis zarucco*	Uncommon
Funereal Duskywing *Erynnis funeralis*	Common
Wild Indigo Duskywing *Erynnis baptisiae*	Uncommon
Common Checkered-Skipper *Pyrgus communis*	Common
Common Streaky-Skipper *Celotes nessus*	Uncommon
Common Sootywing *Pholisora catullus*	Common
Swarthy Skipper *Nastra lherminier*	Uncommon
Julia's Skipper *Nastra julia*	Common
Clouded Skipper *Lerema accius*	Abundant
Least Skipper *Ancyloxypha numitor*	Common
Orange Skipperling *Copaeodes aurantiacus*	Common
Southern Skipperling *Copaeodes minimus*	Common
Fiery Skipper *Hylephila phyleus*	Abundant
Cobweb Skipper *Hesperia metea*	Rare
Green Skipper *Hesperia viridis*	Common
Dotted Skipper *Hesperia attalus*	Uncommon
Meske's Skipper *Hesperia meskei*	Common

Table 4.5 (continued)

Species	Status
Whirlabout *Polites vibex*	Rare
Southern Broken-Dash *Wallengrenia otho*	Uncommon
Northern Broken-Dash *Wallengrenia egeremet*	Rare
Sachem *Atalopedes campestris*	Abundant
Arogos Skipper *Atrytone arogos*	Common
Delaware Skipper *Anatrytone logan*	Uncommon
Zabulon Skipper *Poanes zabulon*	Uncommon
Broad-winged Skipper *Poanes viator*	Rare
Dion Skipper *Euphyes dion*	Common
Dun Skipper *Euphyes vestris metacomet*	Common
Dusted Skipper *Atrytonopsis hianna*	Uncommon
Nysa Roadside-Skipper *Amblyscirtes nysa*	Uncommon
Common Roadside-Skipper *Amblyscirtes vialis*	Common
Celia's Roadside-Skipper *Amblyscirtes celia*	Common
Bell's Roadside-Skipper *Amblyscirtes belli*	Common
Eufala Skipper *Lerodea eufala*	Uncommon
Brazilian Skipper *Calpodes ethlius*	Common
Ocola Skipper *Panoquina ocola*	Common
Yucca Giant-Skipper *Megathymus yuccae*	Uncommon

Abundant = Many individuals of this species be found every visit during normal flight period.

Common = One or more individuals of this species can be found every visit during normal flight period.

Uncommon = One or more individuals of this species can be found on some visits during normal flight period.

Rare = Generally recorded once a year or less frequently.

Vagrant = Has been recorded but is unlikely to be found again.

Fort Worth Nature Center. Fort Worth Nature Center has a wide variety of habitats including woods, fields, brush, marsh, and open water. Because of its diversity, the nature center hosts a large number of butterfly species (table 4.5), ranging from the large Giant, Black, and Tiger Swallowtails to the more diminutive Dion Skipper (*Euphyes dion*) and Henry's Elfin (*Callophrys henrici*). The local Red Satyr can also be found here. The nature center is located on Lake Worth, ten miles northwest of downtown Fort Worth. With 3,500 acres, this urban refuge is the largest in North America and features 25 miles of trails, an interpretive center, and gift shop. The interpretive building is closed on Mondays.

Lake Lewisville. Lake Lewisville has a variety of fields, oak woods, wetlands, and riparian areas. One area especially good for butterflies is located at the north end of Bishop Road, which runs north from Orchard Hill Road. Bishop Road ends in a parking lot. Lake Lewisville is located north of Dallas. Over 65 species have been recorded at the lake; notable sightings have included Great Purple Hairstreaks (*Atlides halesus*), Gorgone and Silvery Checkerspots, and Dusky Roadside-Skippers (*Amblyscirtes alternata*).

Texas Discovery Gardens. Located in Fair Park, Dallas, on Robert B. Cutlum Boulevard, this seven-acre garden includes a large butterfly area behind the building near the greenhouses. The gardens host a nice selection of urban-suburban butterflies, with close to 50 species recorded. Rare highlights have included Large Orange Sulphur (*Phoebis agarithe*), Long-tailed Skipper, and Brazilian Skipper (*Calpodes ethlius*).

Western Plains, Texas

Comanche Trail Park. Comanche Trail Park is located off Interstate 20 on the south side of Odessa. Prime locations for butterflies includes the draws, which have water intermittently, and fields adjacent to groves of trees. The park is especially good for butterflying when the salt cedars are flowering. Regular species include Lyside Sulphur (*Kricogonia lyside*), Southern Dogface, Queen, Vesta and Texan Crescents (*Phycoides vesta, P. texana*), and Common Sootywing (*Pholisora catullus*).

Hogan Park. This grassland and mesquite park has a half-mile trail and offers a good selection of area butterflies. The permanent pond should also be checked. Hogan Park is on the northeast side of Midland; it is off Wadley Road, which can be reached from Fairgrounds Road. Go past the Sibley Learning Center to the Outdoor Learning Center for parking.

North American Butterfly Association July Fourth Counts

A number of locations in our area have hosted July Fourth butterfly counts. In Kansas, these are El Dorado Lake, Harvey County, and Wichita; in Oklahoma, Bryon Hatchery Watchable Wildlife Area, Cleveland County Audubon Society, Great Plains State Park, Nickel Preserve, Keystone Ancient Forest Preserve, Pontotoc Ridge, Tallgrass Prairie National Preserve, Wichita Mountains Wildlife Refuge and Tulsa; and in Texas, Midland and Tarrant Counties. For current information on locations and coordinators, contact the North American Butterfly Association, 4 Delaware Road, Morristown, NJ 07960, or visit the NABA website at www.naba.org.

5

Photographing Butterflies

Taking photographs can be a rewarding way to enjoy a butterfly beyond the moment of its brief physical presence in a garden, meadow, prairie, or woodland. Photography enables you to preserve a facet of the butterfly's beauty and grace. You may see details otherwise not noticed and sharpen your identification skills. Photography allows the confirmation of an unusual visitor to your garden, or even of a species recorded in your county for the first time, without any harm to one of these gentle creatures. Photographing butterflies requires a minimal amount of mental focus and physical dexterity as well as a not so minimal financial commitment.

Camera

The practical choice for butterfly photography is a 35 mm single-lens reflex camera. These cameras provide the reliability, ease of use, and optional equipment required for successful close-up photos. The small size and light weight of SLR cameras are useful for long days in the field or short sessions in the garden.

Autofocus is a primary consideration when purchasing a camera. Improvements in today's autofocus cameras from Nikon, Pentax, Minolta, Canon, and other companies provide the precise and rapid focus qualities needed for photographing butterflies. Autofocus allows more time to deal with other critical problems that need to be solved quickly, such as aperture setting, correct focal point, composition, and background considerations. Sophisticated autofocus cameras also include the option of manual focus, which is useful in some photographic situations.

A primary concern when photographing anything small at close range is obtaining an adequate depth of field so that the butterfly is in focus. To increase depth of field for sharp butterfly photographs, the lens must be stopped down to a small aperture size. Apertures are engraved on the lens barrel and are referred to as F-stops, with the small-sized apertures having higher numbers. In other words, F 22 is a smaller aperture and will provide more depth of field than F 16.

Many of today's 35 mm cameras not only offer traditional manual exposure, in which the photographer sets both aperture and shutter speed based on the camera's light meter, but also various modes of autoexposure, including aperture priority, shutter priority, and total autoexposure. Aperture priority allows the photographer to set the aperture manually while the camera sets the shutter speed to obtain the correct exposure. Shutter priority involves setting the shutter manually, and the camera automatically sets the aperture (F-stop). A full autoexposure setting enables the camera to set both aperture and shutter speed automatically. While autoexposure can be advantageous when photographing butterflies, which rarely remain in one place very long, be conscious of the aperture settings.

Lens

Since butterflies range in size from six inches across for the large Eastern Tiger Swallowtail (*Papilio glaucus*) to the diminutive

Western Pygmy-Blue (*Brephidium exile*) of less than one inch, your optics must not only focus at close range but also obtain a reproduction ratio of at least 1:1. The reproduction ratio is the size of the image on film compared to the actual subject size. A reproduction ratio of 1:1 means that the image on film will be the same size as the actual butterfly, and you will be able to obtain a reasonably large image even of small butterflies.

Macro photography of butterflies is possible with a standard telephoto lens that has a focal length between 85 and 200 mm, if used in conjunction with relatively inexpensive extension tubes (rings) to mount between the camera body and lens. Another option for the budget conscious is to use close-up attachment lenses or diopters that screw onto the front of your camera lens like a filter. Photographing a butterfly using a normal lens of 50 mm fitted with close-up attachments is possible but difficult because the close working distance required tends to scare off the insect.

A 90 to 105 mm lens specifically designed for macro or close-up photography will facilitate quality pictures. These optics lessen the chance of frightening the butterfly by allowing you to get an acceptably large image on film from a distance of twelve inches or more. Macro or micro lenses, as well as zoom lenses that have macro capability, are available with even longer focal lengths. Purchase a skylight or ultraviolet filter to protect the front of your lens.

Flash

Using a flash is one approach the photographer can take to get adequate depth of field and have sharp butterfly pictures. The more sophisticated flash units have a focus illuminator that enables the photographer to enter the lepidopteran world of nocturnal moths. A flash can have drawbacks, however. Besides the problems of added weight and bulk, flash units can result in black or dark backgrounds that lack an element of realism, since butterflies are creatures of sunshine. In addition, when shooting from closer than two feet with the flash mounted on the camera's accessory shoe, the flash head cannot be repositioned to light the subject properly.

One solution is to purchase a ringlight that is designed specifically for close-up photography and attaches to the front of the lens. Ringlights can be quite expensive, however, and lack the power and versatility of more traditional flashes.

An inexpensive option for butterfly photographers interested in using a standard flash unit is to acquire a bracket that allows the flash to be mounted forward of its normal position on the camera's accessory shoe. A dual flash bracket is also available, holding two flashes that project out to each side of the camera far enough forward for the light burst to be accurately aimed at the butterfly.

A viable alternative to a mounted flash unit is to use a four- to five-foot-long remote cord that attaches to the camera's accessory shoe at one end and to a flash or speedlight at the other end. Thus you can hold the flash and direct the burst of light exactly where it is needed. Exposure can be varied by changing the distance of the flash in relation to the butterfly. A handheld flash also facilitates additional creativity by giving the photographer the option of directing the light at the butterfly from various angles. Bear in mind that a handheld flash requires a strong wrist, as you must be able to hold the camera with one hand while manipulating the flash with the other. Although fatiguing, this method can achieve striking results.

Film

Flash units allow the butterfly photographer to use transparency (slide) film of ISO 25, 50, or 64. These films provide rich and accurate colors as well as excellent sharpness. Although these slow films with low ISO numbers require more light than do faster films for a satisfactory photograph, a flash will be able to freeze the action and provide proper exposure even when using smaller diameter lens settings.

Using ambient light alone for close-up photography requires film in the range of ISO 100 and higher. Higher speed film allows smaller F-stops and the fast shutter speeds that prevent blurring as a result of butterfly movement, hand trembles, and wind. Many excellent fast films are available on the market today.

Tactics and Techniques

Getting close to a winged insect can be challenging. Although you may sometimes be tempted to do so, never restrain or immobilize a butterfly, as it could be injured and have its brief life shortened. Lightweight, close-focusing binoculars are great to carry while photographing. They allow you to spot your quarry from a distance and provide an enjoyable break from the rigors of photography. When not in use, the binoculars can go into a hip pack along with spare batteries for camera and flash, extra rolls of film, and a copy of *Butterflies of Oklahoma, Kansas, and North Texas.*

Once a butterfly is located, note its behavior. If it is ovipositing or nectaring on the wing, a successful photograph will be extremely difficult. However, if it is basking, nectaring strongly while perched, imbibing sap from a tree wound, or puddling, a slow but steady approach, while staying low, may allow you to get close. Avoid wearing white clothing or shoes. Butterflies will be startled from their perches if a shadow falls across them, so be aware of your orientation to the sun. Don't be surprised if you do everything correctly and the butterfly still makes a hasty exit—as if it has eyes in the back of its head. The butterfly's extraordinary vision is due to its large compound eyes, able to detect color and movement in almost all directions.

Many butterflies exhibit traits of territoriality. Species such as male Zabulon Skippers (*Poanes zabulon*), Question Marks (*Polygonia interrogationis*), and Viceroys (*Limenitis archippus*) return repeatedly to a given perch. If you remain still after these individuals flee, they may return to the same area. Planting a butterfly garden will enhance photo opportunities as well as butterfly observation and will provide insights into natural history.

As you approach a butterfly, you may want to take a few photos from a distance, which can be used later for identification purposes. If you are able to get close, concentrate on manipulating the front of your lens so that it is parallel to as much of the wings and body as possible. Take into consideration that more of the butterfly will be in focus behind the focal point than in the front of it. Make note of background and foreground as you look into the viewfinder and try to achieve the angle needed to remove extraneous elements that may clutter a photograph or even block part of the main subject. Interest is added if parts of the butterfly's anatomy such as the eyes, proboscis, or antennae are clearly shown in the picture.

Keep written records on all photographs. The date and specific locality should always be noted; these are required if the photograph is used to document a county or state record. You may also want to keep a record of film and equipment used plus any other pertinent details. If you have more than a few slides, they can be arranged taxonomically in archival-quality plastic sleeves. A convenient size has pockets for 20 slides and includes prepunched holes so that the pages can be stored in a three-ring binder.

Viewing the natural world through a macro lens is exciting, but expect some failed photographs—unexpected shadows, distracting backgrounds, out-of-focus butterflies, and pictures of empty scenery because the butterfly exited as the shutter was being tripped. Patience is not always a virtue, but it seems to be a necessity when undertaking butterfly-related activities. Setbacks will occur, but there will also be achievements as you capture the vibrant colors of free-flying butterflies. More important, you will develop greater understanding and appreciation of these remarkable creatures of the light.

Identifying Butterflies

D ozens of butterflies are zipping around from flower to flower. Some are large yellow and black butterflies, some are small and brown, all are intriguing. So how do you identify them? The following are some hints and suggestions for learning to identify butterflies.

Identifying a butterfly starts with the first, often brief look. Much can be learned in this first view that can greatly narrow the list of possibilities and help you determine to which group of species the butterfly belongs. Determining the butterfly to species level can occur later with a better view, but first identify the group. The general characteristics (size, color, and habitat preferences) of the butterfly groups found in our area are listed in table 6.1. Note that some members of these groups do not fit the listed characteristics; for example, swallowtails without tails occur south of our area in southern Texas. But generally, pinpointing the group is the best first step.

Table 6.1. General characteristics of butterfly groups that regularly occur in Kansas, Oklahoma, and North Texas

Swallowtails (15–22). All swallowtails are large; some are predominantly dark brown or black and others are predominantly yellow or white with

Table 6.1 (continued)

dark stripes. If seen nectaring, look for the distinctive tails that give this group their name. Swallowtails can be seen flying at all heights and are usually found in sunny, open areas. Swallowtails include several common species easily seen in gardens.

Whites and Sulphurs (23–42). Small to medium-sized butterflies that are found in open sunny areas. True to the group name, whites and sulphurs are white, yellow, or orange; some have extensive brown to black markings. Most fly relatively low, below four feet, but a couple fly high and migrate long distances. Several of the white and sulphur species are common and easily seen in gardens.

Harvester (43). The only member of this group in our area, the Harvester (*Feniseca tarquinius*) is rather uncommon. It is small, predominantly brown to orange, and found in wooded areas. Individuals typically sit on foliage high up but can also land on the ground. The Harvester does not nectar.

Coppers (44–46). A group that is more numerous to the west and north; rare to uncommon in our area. Their name comes from the copper-colored uppersides of many species. These small butterflies are predominantly copper or gray above and whitish with many black or copper-colored spots below. They prefer moist meadows, roadsides, and other open areas and typically fly at heights from ground to eye level.

Hairstreaks (47–54). Small to medium-sized butterflies named for the thin, wispy tails that most species have on their hindwings. Colors range from gray to brown with a variety of spots, stripes, and lines as markings. One species, the Great Purple Hairstreak (*Atlides halesus*), has bright blue, orange, and green colors. Two species, Gray (*Strymon melinus*) and Red-banded Hairstreaks (*Calycopis cecrops*), are common; most are rare to uncommon. Hairstreaks range from knee level to high in the tree-tops. Most hairstreaks occur in sunny openings in woods and brushy areas and frequently perch motionless high in the trees.

Blues (55–62). Small butterflies named for the bright blue upperside typical of most blues, especially males. Some species and many females of other species are predominantly brown or gray above. The underwings are usually white to light gray with various black, orange to red, or white spots. These little gems can be common to abundant and prefer a variety of habitats from dry weedy patches to openings in moist woods to gardens. Males of many blues often congregate on the ground at wet spots but can also occur up to eye level.

Metalmarks (63). Members of this group are rare in our area and a treat to find. Metalmarks are small, predominantly brown butterflies that typically

Table 6.1 (continued)

fly at eye level or lower. Eastern species are found in open wooded areas; southwestern species occur in open scrub.

Snout (64). The only species in its group in our area, the American Snout (*Libytheana carinenta*) is common, occasionally abundant, medium sized, and predominantly brown. On individuals at rest look for the elongated palps ("snout") that give this species its name. It flies from ground level to high in the trees and is a regular garden visitor.

Heliconians and Fritillaries (65–70). Medium to large butterflies which are predominantly orange, brown, and black, often in intricate patterns. Adults fly from ground level to eye level in habitats that range from tallgrass prairie to open woods. Two species, Gulf Fritillary (*Agraulis vanillae*) and Variegated Fritillary (*Euptoieta claudia*), are common garden visitors; the remaining species are uncommon to rare in our area.

True Brushfoots (71–89). This diverse group can be subdivided into the orange, black, and white crescents and checkerspots; the cryptic brown to orange-colored anglewings; the intricately marked brown, orange, and white-colored ladies; and the predominantly brown Common Buckeye (*Junonia coenia*). The ladies and the Common Buckeye also sport striking eyespots. The crescents, checkerspots, ladies and Common Buckeye are inhabitants of weedy areas, gardens, fields, and other open areas; most are common to abundant and most fly from the ground up to eye level. The anglewings prefer woodlands, are common but not numerous, and fly from ground level to the treetops.

Admirals and Relatives (90–92). Another diverse group of butterflies with only a few regularly occurring representatives in our area: Red-spotted Purple (*Limenitis arthemis astyanax*), common in open woods; Viceroy (*Limenitis archippus*), common along water features; and Common Mestra (*Mestra amymone*), rare in the southern part of our area along open woods. All three are medium to large butterflies that occur from the ground to high in the trees. These species are easier to learn as individuals rather than as members of a readily identifiable group. All three species may visit gardens but are not particularly common there.

Leafwing (93). Only one species regularly occurs in our area—Goatweed Leafwing (*Anaea andria*). This large butterfly is well named, as the underside looks like a brown leaf. The upper surface varies from light brown to bright orange. The Goatweed Leafwing does not nectar and prefers fruit, sap, and feces. Look for this large butterfly from the ground to high in the trees. While not rare, this species is always a treat to find.

Emperors (94–95). These unassuming butterflies are brown to tan with a complex array of darker eyespots and lines. What they lack in flash they

Table 6.1 (continued)

make up for in personality, and they can be delightfully tame. They do not nectar but prefer sap and fruit, making them frequent visitors at fruit-based butterfly feeders. Emperors also like perspiration and will land on the back of your neck to get it—be careful what you swat when they are around. Look for these medium-sized butterflies flying from ground level to high in the trees.

Satyrs (96–100). Most members of this group inhabit wooded areas and fly low to the ground in a bouncy, erratic flight that can be surprisingly difficult to keep up with. The predominant color is brown with various numbers of small to large eyespots and rings. Most are small; the Common Wood-Nymph (*Cercyonis pegala*) is the largest member of the group in our area. Many satyrs are common to abundant in proper habitats but not particularly common in the garden.

Milkweed Butterflies (101–103). The Monarch is probably the most famous butterfly in North America. The group also contains the Queen (*Danaus plexippus*), occasionally common in southern Oklahoma and northern Texas, and the Soldier (*Danaus eresimus*), a rare stray in southernmost part of our area. All three species are combinations of orange, mahogany, black, and white. They are large, strong-flying butterflies that occur from close to ground level to very high overhead. Monarchs and Queens prefer open areas and are regular garden visitors

Spread-wing Skippers (104–16). A large, diverse group of small to medium-sized butterflies, including some of the species most difficult to identify—duskywings and cloudywings. Most are various combinations of brown, black, and white. Look for them from the ground to eye level. Some species are common and frequent garden visitors.

Grass-Skippers (117–42). The quintessential "little brown jobs" of the butterfly world—until you get to know them, you can just say "LBJ" with authority, and no one will question you further. Many interesting and beautiful species occur in this group. Most grass-skippers are small brown to black butterflies that fly fast and low (below four feet). Most are found in open sunny areas, including gardens, but a few are found in wooded areas. The grass-skippers includes the Sachem (*Atalopedes campestris*), one of the most common butterflies in our area.

Giant-Skippers (143). Very large skippers that are mostly brown, white, and gray. Most species are rare to uncommon; the only two that occur regularly in our area are Yucca Giant-Skipper (*Megathymus yuccae*) and Strecker's Giant-Skipper (*M. streckeri*). Adults fly from ground level to eye level in grasslands or open woods with yucca.

Having thus determined which section of your field guide to use, the second step is to consult the photographs and descriptions to match the butterfly. Identifying a butterfly to species usually requires a long or close view to see the distinguishing upperwing or underwing markings. Some species are distinctive and readily identifiable; others are more difficult to determine to species.

- Appearance varies with the age and sex of the butterfly and the time of year it is flying. The longer a butterfly has been actively flying, the more worn the wings. As the scales on the wings are lost, some of the distinguishing features will fade or disappear. The males and females of some species are colored quite differently from each other; the Diana Fritillary (*Speyeria diana*) is an extreme example. For most species the differences in appearance between sexes are less pronounced; note, for example, the presence of scent patch on the hindwing of the male Monarch (*Danaus plexippus*). Finally, the appearance of some species varies with the time of year in what are called "forms." On the Dainty Sulphur (*Nathalis iole*), the hindwings of the winter form are darkly colored, while the summer form has light greenish yellow hindwings.

- Size can be a tricky characteristic to use, as some abnormally small individuals occur. The Monarch is almost always larger than the similar-appearing Viceroy (*Limenitis archippus*), but small Monarchs are seen occasionally. On the other hand, if the butterfly you are watching is larger than the descriptions indicate, you can safely eliminate the smaller species.

- The adults of some species emerge from the pupae and fly in a relatively short period of time. This group of adults is known as a brood. Some species, such as the striking Falcate Orangetip (*Anthocharis midea*), have just one brood, which emerges only in early spring. Other one-brooded species emerge at other times of the year. Some species are multi-brooded, and adults of these species can be found for longer periods, from many weeks to months; the Orange Sulphur (*Colias eurytheme*) can be found any month of the year. A number of species migrate into our area each year, and numbers of these species build up during the spring and summer as more individuals arrive and those already here breed and produce new adults. Regardless of why the butterflies are flying, you can use the time of year to narrow the list of possible species. If you find a hairstreak in September that is grayish below, it is not a Soapberry Hairstreak (*Phaeostrymon alcestis*), which flies from May to July. The butterfly is much more likely to be a Gray Hairstreak (*Strymon melinus*), which flies from March to October.

- Grasslands, wetlands, forest, scrub, rocky ravines, and all combinations of these habitats occur in our area. Some species can be found in several kinds of habitats; others are restricted to only one. The Regal Fritillary (*Speyeria idalia*) is found on tallgrass prairie and is highly unlikely ever to occur in woodlands. Many species are associated with specific habitats because that is where their caterpillar host plants occur.

- Another criterion to check is a species' regular range. While individuals can travel out of the species' range (sometimes for spectacularly long distances), the vast majority of individuals of most species stay within their normal range. A light-colored, black-striped swallowtail in Abilene, Texas, is much more likely to be an Eastern Tiger Swallowtail (*Papilio glaucus*) than a Zebra Swallowtail (*Eurytides marcellus*), a species that occurs only in the eastern portion of our region.

Third, learn the common butterflies for your area. The most common butterflies are found in this book—if you know these species, you will have learned 75 percent or more of the butterflies typically seen in Kansas, Oklahoma, and North Texas. Don't worry about identifying every butterfly that you see—some you may just have to watch and enjoy. As you learn more species, the number of unidentified individuals will decrease. Remember that even the experts cannot identify every butterfly they see, especially when confronted with older, worn individuals. The numerous small brown grass-skippers can be particularly difficult. Knowing the common butterflies also allows you to pick out new, unfamiliar species more easily. Some days your favorite spot will be swarming with butterflies and it will be difficult to look at each one. By knowing the common butterflies, you can concentrate instead on those that appear to be new and different.

A great way to gain familiarity with common species is to find a place to visit once a day or once a week and learn the butterflies that occur in the area. The place could be your backyard or a field or garden near your job. It does not matter if the location hosts only a half dozen species—those species are likely to be among the most common and ones you should know. Gardens, nature centers, flowery fields, and areas with mixed fields and shrubs are all good places to visit locally. Is there a spot you can regularly visit over lunch on work days or take the family for an outing on the weekend? Once you learn the common local butterflies, venture forth and visit one of the hotspots listed in chapter 4. At these locations you will probably find new species to enjoy and learn. After that, try another hotspot or strike out on your own and find your own hotspot. At this time you may want to add a couple of books to your library, such as Glassberg's *Butterflies through Binoculars: The East* and/or *Butterflies through Binoculars: The West* (see bibliography for more information) as you may be encountering species which are not found in *Butterflies of Oklahoma, Kansas, and North Texas.*

Beyond Identification

By now you may be hooked on butterflies—what a wonderful problem to have. Here are some ideas for learning yet more about identification and other aspects of the lives of butterflies to improve your butterflying skills.

Take Field Trips. Field trips with experienced butterfliers allow you to pick up their hints for identifying species. You will also learn about other great places to look for butterflies. Organized groups, such as those listed in the Organizations and Resources section of this book, and local nature centers, parks, and preserves may offer field trips. Contact them to find out what they offer. You may want to join one of the groups listed to maximize your enjoyment and learning.

Explore the Web. Many butterfly-related websites are available. Start with general sites such as the United States Geological Survey butterfly site (see Organizations and Resources), which has pictures, range maps, life histories, and many links to related sites. Local websites may provide excellent information on nearby places to visit, upcoming field trips, and butterflies in your immediate area.

Read All You Can. Borrow books from the library and/or buy a second, third, or fourth field guide. Each book is likely to provide a few more hints on identifying species and gives you additional photographs or drawings of butterflies to use. Read the introductory materials in field guides. Take the time to read general information books as well. Many butterflies have unusual and interesting life histories, which can help you understand the species better.

Buy New Binoculars. Great close-focusing binoculars are now available that make butterfly watching easy. Old binoculars are often dark or misaligned, or do not focus closely enough. Brighten up your view with a new pair.

Keep a List. Many butterfliers keep one or more lists: yard, county, and state lists are examples. After a few months of butterflying, compare your list with a field guide. Are there species that the field guide lists as common but that you have not yet seen? If so, you may be overlooking them, especially if they appear similar to another species. Some species may have gone unnoticed because they fly at times of the year you have not been out searching. For example, the beautiful Falcate Orangetip flies in early spring, before most people think about butterflying. Other species may be restricted to certain habitats or parts of the region that you have not yet visited. Daily or trip lists can also be satisfying. From the lists, patterns will emerge. You will know when to start looking for the first Black Swallowtail (*Papilio polyxenes*) of the season or when to expect the numbers of Cloudless Sulphurs (*Phoebis sennae*) to start declining. Some people also keep a life list of all the butterfly species they have ever seen. Review the list occasionally to bring back memories of the first time you saw each species. While some people keep their lists on a computer or in an official checklist, others simply keep it in a special notebook.

Find a Butterflying Companion. If you go out with some-one equally inexperienced, you both can learn the butterflies together. If your companion is familiar with butterflies, you can learn more in a single day than in months of butterflying on your own.

Volunteer Your Time. The North American Butterfly Asso-ciation (see Organizations and Resources) coordinates annual counts in many locations to monitor butterfly populations. New butterfliers are always welcome, and the counts are a great way to learn about butterflies. If no butterfly counts occur in your area—start one. Enlist the help of an expert butterflier for the first year or two, and then you will be ready to run the count yourself. Other organizations can often use the help of a butter-flier. The activities may vary from formal butterfly surveys, such as for the U.S. Fish and Wildlife Service or the Nature Conservancy, to developing a list of butterfly species found in a local public garden. If no opportunities are advertised in your area, create one by approaching the manager of a public property and offering your services.

Teach Butterfly Watching to Others. This may seem an unusual recommendation for a new butterflier, but there is nothing like teaching others to make you learn a subject yourself. Lead a butterfly walk for a local garden club or elementary school class. The limited amount of time on such tours means focusing on the obvious and common species—the ones you have likely mastered already. If your group finds a species you don't know—no problem. Use the mystery species as an opportunity to show everyone how to use a field guide. It can be helpful to start or end walks or talks with a quick review of good butterfly books and general hints on finding and identifying butterflies.

Learning to identify butterflies is a great way to enter the world of butterflies. From the amazing transformation of a caterpillar into an adult butterfly to the spectacular long distance migration of the Monarchs, butterflies display many fascinating biological phenomena. The next time you find a field or a garden alive with butterflies, grab your book and dive in. It will be your guide to the striking and ephemeral beauty of butterflies and your introduction to their wonderful stories.

Appendix

Butterfly Species Recorded in Kansas, Oklahoma, and North Texas

The following species have been recorded in the area covered by this book. An x indicates that the species regularly occurs in some part of the area; some species may be rare but are expected every year. An s indicates that the species is a stray—it does not occur regularly in the area and may not be found every year; some species may never occur in the area again. A dash indicates that the species has not been recorded in the area. Species highlighted in bold are illustrated in this book.

For information on the butterfly species not covered in this book, see the following guides. Eastern portion of our region: *Butterflies through Binoculars: The East* (J. Glassberg, 1999) and *A Field Guide to Eastern Butterflies* (A. Opler, 1998). Western portion of our region: *Butterflies through Binoculars: The West* (J. Glassberg, 2001) and *A Field Guide to Western Butterflies* (A. Opler, 1999). All the butterflies of the continental United States: *The Butterflies of North America* (J. A. Scott, 1986) and *National Audubon Society Field Guide to North American Butterflies* (R. M. Pyle, 1981). More information on all these books can be found in the bibliography.

Species	Kansas	Oklahoma	North Texas
Swallowtails, Family Papilionidae, Subfamily Papilioninae			
White-dotted Cattleheart *Parides alopius*	-	-	s
Pipevine Swallowtail *Battus philenor*	x	x	x
Polydamas Swallowtail *Battus polydamas*	-	-	s

Species	Kansas	Oklahoma	North Texas
Zebra Swallowtail *Eurytides marcellus*	x	x	x
Black Swallowtail *Papilio polyxenes*	x	x	x
Old World Swallowtail *Papilio machaon*	s	-	-
Anise Swallowtail *Papilio zelicaon*	s	-	-
Thoas Swallowtail *Papilio thoas*	s	s	s
Giant Swallowtail *Papilio cresphontes*	x	x	x
Ornythion Swallowtail *Papilio ornythion*	s	-	s
Broad-banded Swallowtail *Papilio astyalus*	-	-	s
Eastern Tiger Swallowtail *Papilio glaucus*	x	x	x
Two-tailed Swallowtail *Papilio multicaudata*	x	x	x
Spicebush Swallowtail *Papilio troilus*	x	x	x
Palamedes Swallowtail *Papilio palamedes*	-	s	x
Ruby-spotted Swallowtail *Papilio anchisiades*	s	-	s

Whites and Sulphurs, Family Pieridae

WHITES, SUBFAMILY PIERINAE

Florida White *Appias drusilla*	s	s	s
Becker's White *Pontia beckerii*	-	s	-
Spring White *Pontia sisymbrii*	-	s	-
Checkered White *Pontia protodice*	x	x	x
Western White *Pontia occidentalis*	s	-	s
Cabbage White *Pieris rapae*	x	x	x
Great Southern White *Ascia monuste*	s	-	s
Giant White *Ganyra josephina*	s	-	-
Olympia Marble *Euchloe olympia*	x	x	x
Falcate Orangetip *Anthocharis midea*	x	x	x

SULPHURS, SUBFAMILY COLIADINAE

Clouded Sulphur *Colias philodice*	x	x	x
Orange Sulphur *Colias eurytheme*	x	x	x
Southern Dogface *Colias cesonia*	x	x	x
White Angled-Sulphur *Anteos chlorinde*	s	s	s
Yellow Angled-Sulphur *Anteos maerula*	-	-	s

Species	Kansas	Oklahoma	North Texas
Cloudless Sulphur *Phoebis sennae*	x	x	x
Orange-barred Sulphur *Phoebis philea*	s	-	s
Apricot Sulphur *Phoebis argante*	-	-	s
Large Orange Sulphur *Phoebis agarithe*	s	s	x
Statira Sulphur *Phoebis statira*	s	-	s
Lyside Sulphur *Kricogonia lyside*	s	s	x
Barred Yellow *Eurema daira*	-	s	x
Mexican Yellow *Eurema mexicana*	x	x	x
Tailed Orange *Eurema proterpia*	s	s	-
Little Yellow *Eurema lisa*	x	x	x
Mimosa Yellow *Eurema nise*	s	-	s
Sleepy Orange *Eurema nicippe*	x	x	x
Dainty Sulphur *Nathalis iole*	x	x	x

Gossamer-wing Butterflies, Family Lycaenidae

HARVESTERS, SUBFAMILY MILETINAE

Species	Kansas	Oklahoma	North Texas
Harvester *Feniseca tarquinius*	x	x	x

COPPERS, SUBFAMILY LYCAENINAE

Species	Kansas	Oklahoma	North Texas
American Copper *Lycaena phlaeas*	x	s	-
Gray Copper *Lycaena dione*	x	x	x
Bronze Copper *Lycaena hyllus*	x	x	-
Purplish Copper *Lycaena helloides*	s	s	-

HAIRSTREAKS, SUBFAMILY THECLINAE

Species	Kansas	Oklahoma	North Texas
Great Purple Hairstreak *Atlides halesus*	s	x	x
Soapberry Hairstreak *Phaeostrymon alcestis*	x	x	x
Coral Hairstreak *Satyrium titus*	x	x	x
Behr's Hairstreak *Satyrium behrii*	-	s	s
Acadian Hairstreak *Satyrium acadica*	x	-	-
Edwards' Hairstreak *Satyrium edwardsii*	s	x	s
Banded Hairstreak *Satryium calanus*	x	x	x
Hickory Hairstreak *Satyrium caryaevorum*	s	-	-

Species	Kansas	Oklahoma	North Texas
Striped Hairstreak *Satyrium liparops*	x	s	x
Oak Hairstreak *Satyrium favonius*	x	x	x
Xami Hairstreak *Callophrys xami*	-	-	s
Frosted Elfin *Callophrys irus*	-	x	x
Henry's Elfin *Callophrys henrici*	x	x	x
Eastern Pine Elfin *Callophrys niphon*	-	x	x
Thicket Hairstreak *Callophrys spinetorum*	-	s	-
Juniper Hairstreak *Callophrys gryneus*	x	x	x
White M Hairstreak *Parrhasius m-album*	s	x	x
Gray Hairstreak *Strymon melinus*	x	x	x
Mallow Scrub-Hairstreak *Strymon istapa*	-	s	-
Red-banded Hairstreak *Calycopis cecrops*	x	x	x
Dusky-blue Groundstreak	s	-	x
Gray Ministreak *Ministrymon azia*	s	-	s
BLUES, SUBFAMILY POLYOMMATINAE			
Western Pygmy-Blue *Brephidium exile*	x	x	x
Cassius Blue *Leptotes cassius*	s	s	s
Marine Blue *Leptotes marina*	x	x	x
Cyna Blue *Zizula cyna*	-	-	s
Ceraunus Blue *Hemiargus ceraunus*	s	s	x
Reakirt's Blue *Hemiargus isola*	x	x	x
Eastern Tailed-Blue *Everes comyntas*	x	x	x
Spring Azure *Celastrina ladon*	x	x	x
Summer Azure *Celastrina neglecta*	x	x	x
Silvery Blue *Glaucopsyche lygdamus*	x	x	x
Melissa Blue *Lycaeides melissa*	x	x	x
Acmon Blue *Plebejus acmon*	x	x	x
Metalmarks, Family Riodinidae			
Little Metalmark *Calephelis virginiensis*	-	x	-
Northern Metalmark *Calephelis borealis*	-	x	-
Swamp Metalmark *Calephelis mutica*	-	x	-

Species	Kansas	Oklahoma	North Texas
Brushfooted Butterflies, Family Nymphalidae			
SNOUTS, SUBFAMILY LIBYTHEINAE			
American Snout *Libytheana carinenta*	x	x	x
HELICONIANS AND FRITILLARIES, SUBFAMILY HELICONIINAE			
Gulf Fritillary *Agraulis vanillae*	x	x	x
Banded Orange Heliconian *Dryadula phaetusa*	s	-	s
Julia Heliconian *Dryas iulia*	s	s	s
Zebra Heliconian *Heliconius charithonia*	s	s	x
Variegated Fritillary *Euptoieta claudia*	x	x	x
Mexican Fritillary *Euptoieta hegesia*	-	-	s
Diana Fritillary *Speyeria diana*	-	x	-
Great Spangled Fritillary *Speyeria cybele*	x	x	-
Aphrodite Fritillary *Speyeria aphrodite*	s	-	-
Regal Fritillary *Speyeria idalia*	x	x	-
Edwards' Fritillary *Speyeria edwardsii*	s	s	-
TRUE BRUSHFOOTS, SUBFAMILY NYMPHALINAE			
Dotted Checkerspot *Polydryas minuta*	-	s	x
Theona Checkerspot *Thessalia theona*	-	-	s
Fulvia Checkerspot *Thessalia fulvia*	x	x	x
Bordered Patch *Chlosyne lacinia*	x	x	x
Crimson Patch *Chlosyne janais*	-	-	s
Rosita Patch *Chlosyne rosita*	-	-	s
Gorgone Checkerspot *Chlosyne gorgone*	x	x	x
Silvery Checkerspot *Chlosyne nycteis*	x	x	x
Tiny Checkerspot *Dymasia dymas*	-	-	s
Elada Checkerspot *Texola elada*	-	-	s
Texan Crescent *Phyciodes texana*	x	x	x
Vesta Crescent *Phyciodes vesta*	x	x	x
Phaon Crescent *Phyciodes phaon*	x	x	x
Pearl Crescent *Phyciodes tharos*	x	x	x
Field Crescent *Phyciodes campestris*	s	s	-

Species	Kansas	Oklahoma	North Texas
Painted Crescent *Phyciodes picta*	x	x	x
Variable Checkerspot *Euphydryas chalcedona*	-	s	-
Baltimore Checkerspot *Euphydryas phaeton*	x	x	s
Question Mark *Polygonia interrogationis*	x	x	x
Eastern Comma *Polygonia comma*	x	x	x
Hoary Comma *Polygonia gracilis*	s	-	-
Gray Comma *Polygonia progne*	x	s	-
Mourning Cloak *Nymphalis antiopa*	x	x	x
Milbert's Tortoiseshell *Nymphalis milberti*	s	-	-
American Lady *Vanessa virginiensis*	x	x	x
Painted Lady *Vanessa cardui*	x	x	x
West Coast Lady *Vanessa annabella*	s	s	s
Red Admiral *Vanessa atalanta*	x	x	x
Common Buckeye *Junonia coenia*	x	x	x
Mangrove Buckeye *Junonia evarete*	-	-	s
Tropical Buckeye *Junonia genoveva*	-	-	s
White Peacock *Anartia jatrophae*	s	-	s
Malachite *Siproeta stelenes*	s	-	-

ADMIRALS AND RELATIVES, SUBFAMILY LIMENITIDINAE

Red-spotted Purple *Limenitis arthemis astyanax*	x	x	x
Viceroy *Limenitis archippus*	x	x	x
Weidemeyer's Admiral *Limenitis weidemeyerii*	-	s	-
California Sister *Adelpha bredowii*	s	s	x
Mexican Bluewing *Myscelia ethusa*	-	-	s
Florida Purplewing *Eunica tatila*	s	-	-
Blue-eyed Sailor *Dynamine dyonis*	-	-	s
Common Mestra *Mestra amymone*	s	s	x
Many-banded Daggerwing *Marpesia chiron*	s	-	-
Ruddy Daggerwing *Marpesia petreus*	s	-	-

Species	Kansas	Oklahoma	North Texas
LEAFWINGS, SUBFAMILY CHARAXINAE			
Tropical Leafwing *Anaea aidea*	s	-	s
Goatweed Leafwing *Anaea andria*	x	x	x
EMPERORS, SUBFAMILY APATURINAE			
Hackberry Emperor *Asterocampa celtis*	x	x	x
Empress Leilia *Asterocampa leilia*	-	-	s
Tawny Emperor *Asterocampa clyton*	x	x	x
SATYRS, SUBFAMILY SATYRINAE			
Southern Pearly-eye *Enodia portlandia*	-	x	x
Northern Pearly-eye *Enodia anthedon*	x	x	-
Creole Pearly-eye *Enodia creola*	s	x	-
Canyonland Satyr *Cyllopsis pertepida*	-	s	-
Gemmed Satyr *Cyllopsis gemma*	x	x	x
Carolina Satyr *Hermeuptychia sosybius*	s	x	x
Georgia Satyr *Neonympha areolata*	-	s	-
Little Wood-Satyr *Megisto cymela*	x	x	x
Red Satyr *Megisto rubricata*	x	x	x
Common Wood-Nymph *Cercyonis pegala*	x	x	x
Ridings' Satyr *Neominois ridingsii*	-	s	-
MONARCHS, SUBFAMILY DANAINAE			
Monarch *Danaus plexippus*	x	x	x
Queen *Danaus gilippus*	x	x	x
Soldier *Danaus eresimus*	-	-	s
Tiger Mimic-Queen *Lycorea cleobaea*	s	-	-

Skippers, Family Hesperiidae

Species	Kansas	Oklahoma	North Texas
SPREAD-WING SKIPPERS, SUBFAMILY PYRGINAE			
Silver-spotted Skipper *Epargyreus clarus*	x	x	x
Broken Silverdrop *Epargyreus exadeus*	-	-	s
Long-tailed Skipper *Urbanus proteus*	s	s	s

Species	Kansas	Oklahoma	North Texas
Dorantes Longtail *Urbanus dorantes*	-	-	s
Golden Banded-Skipper *Autochton cellus*	-	s	s
Hoary Edge *Achalarus lyciades*	x	x	x
Southern Cloudywing *Thorybes bathyllus*	x	x	x
Northern Cloudywing *Thorybes pylades*	x	x	x
Confused Cloudywing *Thorybes confusis*	s	x	x
Acacia Skipper *Cogia hippalus*	-	-	s
Outis Skipper *Cogia outis*	-	x	x
Hayhurst's Scallopwing *Staphylus hayhurstii*	x	x	x
Sickle-winged Skipper *Achlyodes thraso*	s	-	x
Hermit Skipper *Grais stigmatica*	s	-	s
White-patched Skipper *Chiomara asychis*	s	-	-
False Duskywing *Gesta gesta*	-	-	s
Dreamy Duskywing *Erynnis icelus*	-	s	-
Sleepy Duskywing *Erynnis brizo*	x	x	x
Juvenal's Duskywing *Erynnis juvenalis*	x	x	x
Rocky Mountain Duskywing *Erynnis telemachus*	-	x	-
Meridian Duskywing *Erynnis meridianus*	-	-	s
Horace's Duskywing *Erynnis horatius*	x	x	x
Mournful Duskywing *Erynnis tristis*	-	-	s
Mottled Duskywing *Erynnis martialis*	x	x	x
Zarucco Duskywing *Erynnis zarucco*	-	s	s
Funereal Duskywing *Erynnis funeralis*	x	x	x
Columbine Duskywing *Erynnis lucilius*	s	-	-
Wild Indigo Duskywing *Erynnis baptisiae*	x	x	x
Afranius Duskywing *Erynnis afranius*	s	-	-
Persius Duskywing *Erynnis persius*	s	-	-
Common Checkered-Skipper *Pyrgus communis*	x	x	x
Tropical Checkered-Skipper *Pyrgus oileus*	-	-	s
Desert Checkered-Skipper *Pyrgus philetas*	-	-	s

Species	Kansas	Oklahoma	North Texas
Laviana White-Skipper *Heliopetes laviana*	-	-	s
Common Streaky-Skipper *Celotes nessus*	-	s	x
Common Sootywing *Pholisora catullus*	x	x	x
Mexican Sootywing *Pholisora mejicana*	s	-	-
Saltbush Sootywing *Hesperopsis alpheus*	-	-	s
SKIPPERLINGS, SUBFAMILY HETEROPTERINAE			
Russet Skipperling *Piruna pirus*	s	-	-
GRASS-SKIPPERS, SUBFAMILY HESPERIINAE			-
Swarthy Skipper *Nastra lherminier*	s	x	x
Julia's Skipper *Nastra julia*	-	-	s
Neamathla Skipper *Nastra neamathla*	-	-	x
Clouded Skipper *Lerema accius*	s	x	x
Least Skipper *Ancyloxypha numitor*	x	x	x
Orange Skipperling *Copaeodes aurantiacus*	s	x	x
Southern Skipperling *Copaeodes minimus*	-	s	x
Fiery Skipper *Hylephila phyleus*	x	x	x
Rhesus Skipper *Yvretta rhesus*	s	s	s
Carus Skipper *Yvretta carus*	-	s	s
Uncas Skipper *Hesperia uncas*	x	x	x
Ottoe Skipper *Hesperia ottoe*	x	x	x
Leonard's Skipper *Hesperia leonardus*	x	s	-
Pahaska Skipper *Hesperia pahaska*	s	-	s
Cobweb Skipper *Hesperia metea*	x	x	x
Green Skipper *Hesperia viridis*	x	x	x
Dotted Skipper *Hesperia attalus*	x	x	x
Meske's Skipper *Hesperia meskei*	-	-	s
Peck's Skipper *Polites peckius*	x	x	s
Tawny-edged Skipper *Polites themistocles*	x	x	x
Crossline Skipper *Polites origenes*	x	x	x
Whirlabout *Polites vibex*	-	s	x
Southern Broken-Dash *Wallengrenia otho*	x	x	x

Species	Kansas	Oklahoma	North Texas
Northern Broken-Dash *Wallengrenia egeremet*	x	x	x
Little Glassywing *Pompeius verna*	s	x	x
Sachem *Atalopedes campestris*	x	x	x
Arogos Skipper *Atrytone arogos*	x	x	x
Delaware Skipper *Anatrytone logan*	x	x	x
Byssus Skipper *Problema byssus*	x	x	x
Hobomok Skipper *Poanes hobomok*	x	x	-
Zabulon Skipper *Poanes zabulon*	x	x	x
Yehl Skipper *Poanes yehl*	-	s	x
Broad-winged Skipper *Poanes viator*	-	x	x
Dion Skipper *Euphyes dion*	x	x	x
Dukes' Skipper *Euphyes dukesi*	-	-	s
Black Dash *Euphyes conspicua*	-	s	-
Two-spotted Skipper *Euphyes bimacula*	s	-	-
Dun Skipper *Euphyes vestris*	x	x	x
Dusted Skipper *Atrytonopsis hianna*	x	x	x
Viereck's Skipper *Atrytonopsis vierecki*	-	x	x
Simius Roadside-Skipper *Amblyscirtes simius*	-	-	s
Bronze Roadside-Skipper *Amblyscirtes aenus*	s	x	x
Linda's Roadside-Skipper *Amblyscirtes linda*	s	x	-
Oslar's Roadside-Skipper *Amblyscirtes oslari*	x	x	x
Pepper and Salt Skipper *Amblyscirtes hegon*	-	x	-
Texas Roadside-Skipper *Amblyscirtes texanae*	-	-	x
Lace-winged Roadside-Skipper *Amblyscirtes aesculapius*	-	x	x
Nysa Roadside-Skipper *Amblyscirtes nysa*	x	x	x
Dotted Roadside-Skipper *Amblyscirtes eos*	x	x	x
Common Roadside-Skipper *Amblyscirtes vialis*	x	x	x
Celia's Roadside-Skipper *Amblyscirtes celia*	-	-	x
Bell's Roadside-Skipper *Amblyscirtes belli*	x	x	x

Species	Kansas	Oklahoma	North Texas
Dusky Roadside-Skipper *Amblyscirtes alternata*	-	x	x
Eufala Skipper *Lerodea eufala*	x	x	x
Brazilian Skipper *Calpodes ethlius*	s	s	s
Ocola Skipper *Panoquina ocola*	-	x	x
GIANT-SKIPPERS, SUBFAMILY MEGATHYMINAE			
Yucca Giant-Skipper *Megathymus yuccae*	x	x	x
Strecker's Giant-Skipper *Megathymus streckeri*	x	x	x

Glossary

Words in italics are defined elsewhere in the glossary.

Abdomen. Third and last region of an insect's body furthest away from the head. The abdomen contains digestive and reproductive organs but does not have legs attached.

Alkaloids. Chemicals some plants produce, typically poisonous.

Androconial scales. Scales that produce *pheromones* and are sometimes clustered into patches such as the *stigma* on most grass-skippers. Androconial scales are also known as the scent scales or the sex scales.

Antenna (plural: **antennae**). A pair of sensory organs attached to the front of the head. On butterflies the antennae are long and needle-like, terminating in a thickened knob known as the *antennal club*. The knob may have an additional hook at the end, such as that which occurs on skippers.

Antennal club. The thickened knobby end of the *antenna*.

Apex. The outer tip of the wing along the leading edge.

Apical. Areas of the wings farthest away from the body.

Aposematic. Having colors that warn predators to leave them alone.

Automimicry. The protection one member of a species gains from being associated by predators with unpalatable members of the same species.

Basal. Areas of the wings close to the body.

Batesian mimic. A palatable species that gains protection from mimicking an unpalatable one.

Border. A band of markings or color along a wing margin.

Brood. All of the offspring that hatch, and usually mature, at one time from one set of parents that also matured at one time.

Butterfly. A member of the order Lepidoptera, which also contains *moths* and *skippers*. Butterflies are similar to skippers and usually lumped together with them but have some anatomical differences. In this book, the word *butterfly* often refers to both butterflies and skippers.

Caterpillar. The second stage in a butterfly's life cycle. Also known as *larva* or larval stage.

Cell. The central area of the wing, bordered by wing veins.

Cell-end bar. An elongated spot, usually dark, along the vein at the outer edge of a wing cell.

Chrysalis. The naked *pupa* with a hardened outer shell of a butterfly; the life stage following the *caterpillar* or larval stage.

Cocoon. A silken covering of the *pupa*, spun by the *larvae* of a few butterflies and many moths prior to *pupation*.

Costa or **costal margin.** The leading edge of the forewing.

Cremaster. An appendage with hooks at the end that allows a butterfly *larva* emerging from its final larval skin to hold onto a support while it forms a *chrysalis*.

Crown. Top of the head.

Diapause. A temporary slowdown in development. Often used to allow the organism to survive unfavorable environmental conditions.

Disc. The central portion of the wing including but larger than the *cell*.

Dorsal. The dorsal surface is the upperside of the wings when the butterfly has its wings outstretched.

Ecdysis. The process of a *larva* shedding its skin.

Eclosure. Emergence ("hatching") of an adult butterfly from its *chrysalis*.

Estivate. To become dormant for a lengthy period of time, usually during hot, dry weather, to allow the organism to survive unfavorable environmental conditions.

Exoskeleton. The hard outer covering of an *invertebrate*.

Extinct. There are no living members of an extinct species.

Extirpate. To eliminate a species from a local area.

Frass. Pellets of *caterpillar* waste.

Ectothermic. Describes animals that need warm temperatures to move around.

Entomology. The scientific study of insects.

Forewings. The front, leading pair of the wings closest to the head.

Fringes. Scales that extend outward from the edges of the wings.

Ground color. The general or background color of the wing.

Hilltopping. The process of butterflies concentrating on or near the tops of hills searching for mates.

Hindwing. The back pair of wings farthest from the head.

Honey glands. Glands on a *caterpillar*, typically from the family Lycaenidae, for producing honeydew, a sugary liquid the larvae produce to nourish the ants that tend these *larvae* in a relationship known as *myrmecophily*.

Host plants. Plants upon which *larvae* feed.

Imago. The adult insect.

Instar. Stages of growth for a *larva*. Butterfly *caterpillars* have four or more instars, five being common.

Invertebrates. Animals that do not have a backbone. Butterflies are invertebrates.

Larva (plural: **larvae**). The second stage of a butterfly's life cycle. The larva is usually elongated and variously colored. Also known as the *caterpillar*.

Lepidopteran. Refers to the order Lepidoptera, a group of insects characterized by having tiny scales covering the wings. Lepidoptera include *butterflies*, *skippers*, and *moths*.

Lepidopterist. Scientist who studies butterflies and moths, members of the order Lepidoptera.

Margin. The outer edge of the wing, farthest from the body.

Median. Areas of the wings about halfway between the body and the outer *margin*.

Metamorphosis. To change form. Butterflies undergo metamorphosis three times during their life cycle: egg to *larva* to *pupa* to adult.

Micropyle. The area at the top of the egg that allows sperm to enter.

Mimic. A species that closely resembles another species, which is typically unpalatable.

Mimicry. The process in which one species resembles another unpalatable species, reducing the likelihood that the mimicking species will be eaten by predators. See also *Batesian mimic*, *Müllerian mimic*, and *automimicry*.

Monophagous. A butterfly species in which the larvae use only one host plant species.

Moth. A member of the order Lepidoptera, which also contains *butterflies* and *skippers*. As compared to butterflies, moths typically have feathery or flagellated antennae and are heavy bodied. Although there are some colorful day-flying moths, most moths fly at night and butterflies fly during the day.

Müllerian mimic. An unpalatable species that gains additional protection from mimicking another unpalatable species.

Myrmecophily. The relationship between ants and butterflies in which ants tend and protect caterpillars in exchange for the caterpillars providing the ants with a sweet substance from abdominal glands.

Nymphalids. Members of the family Nymphalidae.

Oligophagous. A butterfly species in which the larvae use only a few closely related plants in the same family as hosts.

Osmaterium. A forked, brightly colored organ at the front of the thorax of swallowtail *caterpillars*. The osmaterium emits a chemical to repel predators.

Outer angle. Area of the hindwing where the outer margin turns inward toward the body. Eye spots or *thecla spots* are often located at the outer angle.

Oviposit. To lay an egg.

Parasitoid. Animals such as some wasps and flies that lay their eggs in the bodies of other animals. Numerous insects are parasitoids of butterfly *larvae*.

Pheromone. Scented chemical that attracts the opposite sex to facilitate mating. Butterfly pheromones come from specialized scales on the wings called *androconial* scales.

Pierids. Members of the family Pieridae.

Polyphagous. A butterfly species in which the larvae use many plant species as hosts.

Polyhedrosis virus. A virus that attacks and kills butterfly larvae or pupae.

Postmedian. Areas of wings farther out from the body than the *median*.

Predators. Animals that eat other animals for food. Predators of butterflies include ants, assassin bugs, praying mantises, spiders, birds, etc.

Proboscis. The tubular organ through which adult butterflies take up nectar.

Protandry. The phenomenon in some species whereby males *eclose* before females.

Puddling. A gathering of butterflies, usually males, at a wet spot.

Pupa (plural: **pupae**). The naked, hard-shelled stage of a butterfly, which follows the *caterpillar* or *larval* stage. Also known as the *chrysalis*.

Pupate, pupation. The process of forming a *pupa*.

Resident. A butterfly species that breeds and lives within a specific area.

Riparian. Refers to the plants and animals that live along streams and rivers.

Skipper. A member of the order Lepidoptera, which also contains *moths* and *butterflies*. Skippers are similar to butterflies and usually lumped together with them but have some anatomical differences. In this book, the word *butterfly* generally refers to both butterflies and skippers.

Spermatophore. A packet of sperm passed from the male to the female during mating.

Stigma. A highly visible concentration of androconial scales; distinctive on some grass-skippers.

Subapical. Areas of the wings slightly closer to the body than the apex.

Submarginal. Areas of the wings slightly closer to the body than the outside edge of the wing.

Teneral period. The period immediately after *eclosure*, up to several hours long. During this time the wings are expanding and hardening.

Thecla spot (mark). A black and orange or red spot on the outer angle of the hindwing near the tails of hairstreaks.

Thermoregulation. The process by which a butterfly regulates its temperature.

Thorax. The second or middle region of an insect's body, bearing the legs and wings.

Trapline. A series of known nectar and/or pollen sources that are visited regularly.

Veins. Thin raised lines on the wings that serve to support the wings.

Ventral. The ventral surface is the underside of the wings when the butterfly has its wings outstretched.

Organizations and Resources

Nature Conservancy
4245 North Fairfax Drive, Suite 100
Arlington, VA 22203
www.nature.org

Oklahoma Chapter
2727 East 21st Street, Suite 102
Tulsa, OK 74114
(918) 585-1117

Kansas Chapter
700 S.W. Jackson, Suite 804
Topeka, KS 66603
(785) 233-4400

Texas Chapter
P.O. Box 1440
San Antonio, TX 78295
(210) 224-8774

An international conservation organization, the Nature Conservancy promotes biological diversity through restoration and protection of important habitat. Some of the more than fourteen hundred preserves it owns are located in the southern plains.

North American Butterfly Association
4 Delaware Road
Morristown, NJ 07960
(973) 285-0907 (phone)
(973) 285-0936 (fax)
www.naba.org

The NABA quarterly *American Butterflies* exposes members to all aspects of butterflying, including identification, species accounts, biology, gardening, hotspots, butterfly count highlights, and conservation. NABA also publishes *Butterfly Gardener* and promotes the annual Fourth of July Butterfly Counts in the United States, Mexico, and Canada.

Xerces Society

4828 S.E. Hawthorne Boulevard
Portland, OR 97215
(503) 232-6639 (phone)
(503) 233-6794 (fax)
info@xerces.org
www.xerces.org

The Xerces Society focuses on invertebrate conservation. It publishes *Wings* twice a year, containing illuminating essays on butterflies and other invertebrates.

Lepidopterists' Society

c/o Los Angeles County Museum of Natural History
900 Exposition Boulevard
Los Angeles, CA 90007-4057

The Lepidopterists' Society provides information on moths and butterflies in *News of the Lepidopterists' Society* and *Journal of the Lepidopterists' Society*. The society also publishes annual summaries of new state records for moths and butterflies.

Northern Prairie Wildlife Research Center

www.npwc.usgs.gov/resource/distr/lepid/bflyusa/bflyusa.htm

This website has up-to-date lists of all butterflies recorded in each state as well as county records. All new records must be documented with date and specific locality accompanying the specimen or photograph. Biological information is provided for each butterfly species and most have one or more accompanying photographs.

Bibliography

Ajilvsgi, Geyata. 1990. *Butterfly Gardening for the South*. Dallas: Taylor Publishing Co.

Black, Scott H., Matthew Shepard, and Melody M. Allen. 2001. Endangered invertebrates: The case for greater attention to invertebrate conservation. *Endangered Species Update* (University of Michigan) 18(2):42–50.

Brewer, Jo, and Dave Winter. 1986. *Butterflies and Moths: A Companion to Your Field Guide*. New York: Phalarope Books.

Brower, Andrew V. Z., and Karen R. Sime. 1998. A reconsideration of mimicry and aposematism in caterpillars of the *Papilio machaon* group. *Journal of the Lepidopterists' Society* 52(2):206–212.

Brower, Lincoln P. 1969. Ecological chemistry. *Scientific American* 220(2):22–29.

———. 1995. Understanding and misunderstanding the migration of the Monarch Butterfly (Nymphalidae) in North America: 1857–1995. *Journal of the Lepidopterists' Society* 49(4):304–385.

———. 2001. Canary in the cornfield. *Orion* 20(2):32–41.

Brower, Lincoln, and Stephen B. Malcolm. 1989. Endangered phenomena. *Wings* 14(2):3–9.

Buchmann, Stephen L., and Gary P. Nabhan. 1996. *The Forgotten Pollinators*. Washington, D.C.: Island Press.

Calvert, William, and Lincoln P. Brower. 1979. Mortality of the Monarch butterfly: Avian predation at five overwintering sites in Mexico. *Science* 204:847–851.

Conaway, Charles F. 1997. Definitive destination: Pontotoc ridge preserve, Oklahoma. *American Butterflies* 5(2):4–13.

Cushman, J. Hall, and Dennis D. Murphy. 1993. Susceptibility of lycaenid butterflies to endangerment. *Wings* 17(2):16–21.

Douglas, Matthew. 1986. *The Lives of Butterflies*. Ann Arbor: University of Michigan Press.

Ehrlich, Paul R., and Peter H. Raven. 1967. Butterflies and plants. *Scientific American* 216:104–113.

Ely, Charles A., Marvin D. Schwilling, and Marvin E. Rolfs. 1986. *An Annotated List of the Butterflies of Kansas*. Hays: Fort Hays State University.

Emmel, Thomas, Marc C. Minno, and Boyce A. Drummond. 1992. *Florissant Butterflies: A Guide to the Fossil and Present-Day Species of Central Colorado*. Stanford, Calif.: Stanford University Press.

Feltwell, John. 1986. *The Natural History of Butterflies*. New York: Facts on File.

Ferris, Clifford D., and F. Martin Brown. 1981. *Butterflies of the Rocky Mountain States*. Norman: University of Oklahoma Press.

Field, William D., Cyril F. dos Passos, and John H. Masters. 1974. A Bibliogaphy of the Catalogs, Lists, Faunal, and Other Papers on the Butterflies of North American North of Mexico Arranged by State and Province (Lepidoptera: Rhopalocera). *Smithsonian Contributions to Zoology* no. 157. 104 pp.

Fitzgerald, Terrence D. 1995. Caterpillars roll their own. *Natural History* 104(4): 30–36.

Freeman, Craig C., and Eileen K. Schofield. 1991. *Roadside Wildflowers of the Southern Great Plains*. Lawrence: University Press of Kansas.

Glassberg, Jeffrey. 1999. *Butterflies through Binoculars: The East*. New York: Oxford University Press.

———. 2001. *Butterflies through Binoculars: The West*. New York: Oxford University Press.

Glassberg, Jeffrey, Paul A. Opler, Robert M. Pyle, and Robert K. Robbins. 1998. There's no need to release butterflies—they're already free. *American Butterflies* 6(1):2.

Griffiths, Mark. 1994. *Index of Garden Plants*. Portland, Ore.: Timber Press.

Heitzman, Richard. 1965. The life history of *Problema byssus* (Hesperiidae). *Journal of the Lepidopterists' Society* 19(2):77–81.

Heitzman, J. Richard, and Joan E. Heitzman. 1987. *Butterflies and Moths of Missouri*. Jefferson City: Conservation Commission of the State of Missouri.

Howe, William H. 1975. *The Butterflies of North America*. Garden City, N.Y.: Doubleday.

Hunter, Carl G. 1984. *Wildflowers of Arkansas*. Little Rock: Ozark Society Foundation.

Kelly, Liesl, and Diane M. Debinski. 1998. Relationship of host plant density to size and abundance of the Regal Fritillary, *Speyeria idalia* Drury (Nymphalidae). *Journal of the Lepidopterists' Society* 52(3):262–276.

Klots, Alexander B. 1951. *A Field Guide to the Butterflies of North America, East of the Great Plains*. Boston: Houghton Mifflin.

Neck, Raymond W. 1996. *A Field Guide to Butterflies of Texas*. Houston: Gulf Publishing.

Nelson, John. 1979. A preliminary checklist of the skippers and butterflies of Oklahoma. *Proceedings of the Oklahoma Academy of Sciences* 59:41–46.

New, T. R. 1997. *Butterfly Conservation*, 2nd edition. Melbourne: Oxford University Press.

North American Butterfly Association. 2001. *Checklist and English Names of North American Butterflies*, 2nd edition. Morristown, N.J.: North American Butterfly Association.

Opler, Paul A. 1998. *A Field Guide to Eastern Butterflies*. Boston: Houghton Mifflin.

———. 1999. *A Field Guide to Western Butterflies*. Boston: Houghton Mifflin.

Opler, Paul A., and George O. Krizek. 1984. *Butterflies East of the Great Plains*. Baltimore: Johns Hopkins University Press.

Orwig, Tim, and Dennis Schlicht. 1999. The last of the Iowa skippers. *American Butterflies* 7(1):4–12.

Owen, Denis. 1980. *Camouflage and Mimicry*. Oxford: Oxford University Press.

Parmesan, C., N. Ryrholm, C. Stefanescu, J. Hill, C. Thomas, H. Descimon, B. Huntley, L. Kaila, J. Kullberg, T. Tammaru, W. Tennent, J. Thomas, and M. Warren. 1999. Poleward shifts in geographical ranges of butterfly species associated with regional warming. *Nature* 399:579–583.

Peterson, Merrill. 1994. Caterpillars and their hired guns. *American Butterflies* 2(4):25–28.

Pyle, Robert M. 1981. *National Audubon Society Field Guide to North American Butterflies*. New York: Alfred Knopf.

————. 1992. *A Handbook for Butterfly Watchers*. Boston: Houghton Mifflin.

————. 1997. Burning bridges. *Wings* 20(1):22–23.

————. 1999. *Chasing Monarchs*. Boston: Houghton Mifflin.

Robbins, Robert. 1993. False heads: The real tale. *American Butterflies* 1(4):19–22.

Ross, Edward S. 1999. I like caterpillars. *Wings* 22(2):3–6.

Rothschild, Miriam. 1967. Mimicry. *Natural History* 76(2):44–51.

Rutowski, Ronald L. 1998. Mating strategies in butterflies. *Scientific American* 279(1):64–69.

Schappert, Phil. 2000. *A World for Butterflies*. Buffalo, N.Y.: Firefly Books.

Schwilling, Marvin D., and Charles A. Ely. 1991. Checklist of Kansas butterflies. *Kansas School Naturalist* 37(4).

Scott, James A. 1986. *The Butterflies of North America*. Stanford, Calif.: Stanford University Press.

Scudder, Samuel H. 1895. *Frail Children of the Air*. Boston: Houghton Mifflin.

Stamp, Nancy E. 1984. Foraging behavior of Tawny Emperor caterpillars (Nymphalidae: *Asterocampa clyton*). *Journal of the Lepidopterists' Society* 38(3):186–191.

Stokes, Donald, and Lillian Stokes. 1991. *The Butterfly Book*. Boston: Little Brown.

Sutton, Patricia T., and Clay Sutton. 1999. *How to Spot Butterflies*. Boston: Houghton Mifflin.

Swengel, Ann. 1993. Regal Fritillary: Prairie royalty. *American Butterflies* 1(1):4–9.

————. 1997. *Straight Talk about Butterfly Population Biology*. Morristown, N.J.: North American Butterfly Association.

————. 1998. *Managing for Butterflies in Prairie*. Morristown, N.J.: North American Butterfly Association.

Taylor, R. John, and Constance Taylor. 1989. *An Annotated List of the Ferns, Fern Allies, Gymnosperms, and Flowering Plants of Oklahoma*. Durant: Southeastern Oklahoma State University.

Tekulsky, Matthew. 1985. *The Butterfly Garden*. Boston: Harvard Common Press.

Tveten, John, and Gloria Tveten. 1996. *Butterflies of Houston.* Austin: University of Texas Press.

Tyler, Hamilton A., Keith S. Brown, and Kent H. Wilson. 1994. *Swallowtail Butterflies of the Americas.* Gainesville, Fla.: Scientific Publishers.

Wagner, David. 1995. Rearing Regals for reintroduction: Playing the odds but still losing ground. *American Butterflies* 3(2):19–23.

Weed, Clarence M. 1926. *Butterflies.* Garden City, N.Y.: Doubleday.

Weiss, Martha. 2000. Brainy butterflies. *Natural History* 109(6):38–41.

Williams, Barry. 1999. Save the Regals--now. *American Butterflies* 7(4):16–25.

Williams, C. B. 1937. Butterfly travelers. *National Geographic* 71(5):568–585.

———. 1958. *Insect Migration.* New York: Macmillan.

Wilson, Edward O. 1987. The little things that run the world. *Wings* 12(3):4–8.

Wright, Amy B. 1993. *Peterson First Guide to Caterpillars of North America.* Boston: Houghton Mifflin.

Xerces Society/Smithsonian Institution. 1998. *Butterfly Gardening.* San Francisco: Sierra Club Books.

Yoon, Carol K. 1998. On the trail of the Monarch, with the aid of chemistry. *New York Times*, December 29, 148:F5.

———. 2001, When biological control gets out of control. *New York Times*, March 6, 150:F3.

Photo Credits
and Information

All photographs were taken by Walter B. Gerard, except as indicated. Walter used Nikon N90S and F100 cameras equipped with Nikkor 105 mm micro Nikkor lens and SB-21 ring light. Film was Fuji Velvia 50.

Fig. I.2: 6/9/85, Osage Co., Okla.

Fig. I.3: 6/96, Cimarron Co., Okla., **J. Dole**

Pipevine Swallowtail: *Upperside*, 5/19/02, Oxley Nature Center, Tulsa Co., Okla. *Underside*, 7/6/99, Tulsa, Tulsa Co., Okla.

Zebra Swallowtail: *Upperside*, spring form 6/17/00, Pettigrew State Park, Washington Co., N.C., **R. Emmitt.** *Underside*, summer form, date unknown, Ft. Gibson, Muskogee Co., Okla., **J. McMahon.**

Black Swallowtail: *Upperside*, male 3/24/00, Tulsa, Tulsa Co., Okla. *Upperside*, female 8.7/01, Tulsa, Tulsa Co., Okla. *Underside*, 8/11/99, Tulsa, Tulsa Co., Okla.

Giant Swallowtail: *Upperside*, 10/24/99, near Roma, Starr Co., Tex. *Underside*, 7/24/99, Tallgrass Prairie Preserve, Osage Co., Okla.

Eastern Tiger Swallowtail: *Upperside*, yellow form 4/15/01, Oxley Nature Center, Tulsa Co., Okla. *Underside*, yellow form 6/6/00, Pontotoc Preserve, Pontotoc Co., Okla. *Upperside*, black form 7/24/00, Pontotoc Preserve, Pontotoc Co., Okla. *Underside*, black form 7/24/99, Tallgrass Prairie Preserve, Osage Co., Okla.

Spicebush Swallowtail: *Upperside*, male 6/26/99, Ottawa Co., Okla. *Underside*, 7/11/01, Nickel Preserve, Cherokee Co., Okla.

Checkered White: *Upperside*, male 5/19/01, Oxley Nature Center, Tulsa Co., Okla. *Underside*, male 6/16/01, Pontotoc Preserve, Pontotoc Co., Okla. *Upperside*, female 5/19/99, Tulsa, Tulsa Co., Okla. *Underside*, female 11/12/99, Tulsa, Tulsa Co., Okla.

Cabbage White: *Upperside*, male 10/14/01, Tulsa Garden Center, Tulsa Co., Okla. *Upperside*, female 10/14/01, Tulsa Garden

Center, Tulsa Co., Okla. *Underside*, 5/29/00, Tulsa, Tulsa Co., Okla.

Olympia Marble: *Upperside*, 3/20/82, Bixby, Tulsa Co., Okla. (pinned specimen collected by J. Nelson). *Underside*, 3/20/82, Bixby, Tulsa Co., Okla. (pinned specimen collected by J. Nelson).

Falcate Orangetip: *Upperside*, male, 4/24/98, Talimena Drive, LeFlore Co., **J. Dole.** *Upperside*, female 4/14/01, Oxley Nature Center, Tulsa Co., Okla. *Underside*, female 4/19/99, Baker Wetland, Lincoln Co., Okla.

Clouded Sulphur: *Underside*, male 7/8/99, Rouge River State Game Area, Mich., Kent Co., **J. Dole.**

Orange Sulfur: *Underside*, female orange form 5/12/01, Pontotoc Preserve, Pontotoc Co., Okla. *Underside*, female white form 11/9/99, Tulsa, Tulsa Co., Okla.

Southern Dogface: *Underside*, summer form 10/22/99, Mission, Hidalgo Co., Tex. *Underside*, fall form 10/21/99, Santa Anna National Wildlife Refuge, Hidalgo Co., Tex.

Cloudless Sulphur: *Underside*, male 8/14/99, Stillwater, Payne Co., Okla., **J. Dole.** *Underside*, female 7/24/99, Tallgrass Prairie Preserve, Osage Co., Okla.

Large Orange Sulphur: *Underside*, female 10/21/99, Santa Anna National Wildlife Refuge, Hidalgo Co., Tex. *Underside*, female white form 10/21/99, Santa Anna National Wildlife Refuge, Hidalgo Co., Tex.

Mexican Yellow: *Underside*, 7/11/99, Pontotoc Preserve, Pontotoc Co., Okla.

Little Yellow: *Underside*, yellow form 9/20/98, Tallgrass Prairie Preserve, Osage Co., Okla. *Underside*, female white form 7/11/99, Pontotoc Preserve, Pontotoc Co., Okla.

Sleepy Orange: *Upperside*, 6/25/96, Tallgrass Prairie Preserve, Osage Co., Okla. *Underside*, summer form 8/29/99, Stillwater, Payne Co., Okla.

Dainty Sulphur: *Underside*, summer form 9/20/98, Tallgrass Prairie Preserve, Osage Co., Okla. *Underside*, winter form 11/7/99, Tulsa, Tulsa Co., Okla.

Harvester: *Underside*, 4/10/98, Tulsa, Tulsa Co., Okla.

Gray Copper: *Upperside*, male 5/19/01, Oxley Nature Center, Tulsa Co., Okla. *Underside*, 5/19/01, Oxley Nature Center, Tulsa Co., Okla.

Bronze Copper: *Upperside*, female 10/17/97, Baker Wetland, Lincoln Co., Okla. *Underside*, 10/17/97, Baker Wetland, Lincoln Co., Okla.

Great Purple Hairstreak: *Underside*, 6/6/00, Pontotoc Preserve, Pontotoc Co., Okla.

Soapberry Hairstreak: *Underside*, 6/15/00, Pontotoc Preserve, Pontotoc Co., Okla.

Coral Hairstreak: *Underside*, 6/6/00, Pontotoc Preserve, Pontotoc Co., Okla.

Banded Hairstreak: *Underside*, 5/28/00, Ottawa Co., Okla.

Henry's Elfin: *Underside*, 4/2/98, Baker Wetland, Lincoln Co., Okla.

Juniper Hairstreak: *Underside*, 4/98, Stillwater, Payne Co., Okla., J. Dole.

Gray Hairstreak: *Upperside*, female 7/3/97, Tallgrass Prairie Preserve, Osage Co., Okla. *Underside*, 6/5/97, Sparks Wetland, Lincoln Co., Okla.

Red-banded Hairstreak: *Underside*, 9/6/99, Tulsa, Tulsa Co., Okla.

Western Pygmy-Blue: *Underside*, 7/4/00, Glass Mountains, Major Co., Okla.

Marine Blue: *Underside*, 7/4/99, Wichita Mountains National Wildlife Refuge, Comanche Co., Okla., J. Dole.

Reakirt's Blue: *Upperside*, male 7/11/99, Pontotoc Preserve, Pontotoc Co., Okla. *Upperside*, female 4/15/01, Oxley Nature Center, Tulsa Co., Okla. *Underside*, 7/11/99, Pontotoc Preserve, Pontotoc Co., Okla.

Eastern Tailed-Blue: *Upperside*, male 6/14/99, Pontotoc Preserve, Pontotoc Co., Okla. *Underside*, 7/26/98, Tallgrass Prairie Preserve, Osage Co., Okla.

Spring Azure: *Underside*, 5/15/01, Oxley Nature Center, Tulsa Co., Okla.

Summer Azure: *Underside*, 7/3/99, Tallgrass Prairie Preserve, Osage Co., Okla., J. Dole.

Melissa Blue: *Upperside*, female 7/20/02, Lookout Mountain,

Ochoco National Forest, Crook Co., Ore. *Underside*, 7/20/02, Lookout Mountain, Ochoco National Forest, Crook Co., Ore.

Swamp Metalmark: *Upperside*, 5/25/01, Ottawa Co., Okla. *Underside*, 5/25/01, Ottawa Co., Okla.

American Snout: *Upperside*, 10/20/99, Bentsen–Rio Grande State Park, Hidalgo Co., Tex. *Underside*, 8/11/99, Tulsa, Tulsa Co., Okla.

Gulf Fritillary: *Upperside*, 7/15/97, Tallgrass Prairie Preserve, Osage Co., Okla. *Underside*, 8/14/99, Pontotoc Preserve, Pontotoc Co., Okla.

Variegated Fritillary: *Upperside*, 10/1/96, Tallgrass Prairie Preserve, Osage Co., Okla. *Underside*, 8/14/99, Pontotoc Preserve, Pontotoc Co., Okla.

Diana Fritillary: *Upperside*, male 7/1/00, Montgomery Co., Va., **R. Emmitt.** *Underside*, male 7/1/00, Montgomery Co., Va., **R. Emmitt.** *Upperside*, female 6/18/98, Cucumber Creek, LeFlore Co., Okla. *Underside*, female 7/1/00, Montgomery Co., Va., **R. Emmitt.**

Great Spangled Fritillary: *Upperside*, 6/18/98, Cucumber Creek, LeFlore Co., Okla. *Underside*, 7/11/01, Nickel Preserve, Cherokee Co., Okla.

Regal Fritillary: *Upperside*, 7/27/99, McCarthy Lake Wildlife Management Area, Minn., **J. Dole.** *Underside*, 7/27/99, McCarthy Lake Wildlife Management Area, Minn., **J.Dole.**

Bordered Patch: *Upperside*, 10/28/99, Santa Anna National Wildlife Refuge, Hidalgo Co., Tex. *Underside*, 10/24/99 Bentsen–Rio Grande State Park, Hidalgo Co., Tex.

Gorgone Checkerspot: *Upperside*, 6/16/01, Pontotoc Preserve, Pontotoc Co., Okla. *Underside*, 6/6/00, Pontotoc Preserve, Pontotoc Co., Okla.

Silvery Checkerspot: *Upperside*, 7/11/99, Pontotoc Preserve, Pontotoc Co., Okla. *Underside*, 5/14/00, Pontotoc Preserve, Pontotoc Co., Okla.

Texan Crescent: *Upperside*, 10/28/98, Santa Anna National Wildlife Refuge, Hidalgo Co., Tex. *Upperside*, 11/7/99, Tulsa Garden Center, Tulsa Co., Okla. *Underside*, 10/26/99, Santa Anna National Wildlife Refuge, Hildago Co., Tex.

Phaon Crescent: *Upperside*, 10/18/96, Tallgrass Prairie Preserve, Osage Co., Okla. *Underside*, 10/18/96, Tallgrass Prairie Preserve, Osage Co., Okla.

Pearl Crescent: *Upperside*, 6/18/98, Cucumber Creek, LeFlore Co., Okla. *Underside*, 6/6/01, Oxley Nature Center, Tulsa Co., Okla. *Underside*, summer form 7/24/99, Tallgrass Prairie Preserve, Osage Co., Okla.

Painted Crescent: *Upperside*, 6/3/97, Beaver Wildlife Management Area, Beaver Co., Okla. (pinned specimen collected by J. Nelson and C. Conaway). *Underside*, 6/3/97, Beaver Wildlife Management Area, Beaver Co., Okla. (pinned specimen collected by J. Nelson and C. Conaway).

Baltimore Checkerspot: *Upperside*, 5/25/01, Ottawa Co., Okla. *Underside*, 5/28/00, Ottawa Co., Okla.

Question Mark: *Upperside*, winter form 10/13/96, Tallgrass Prairie Preserve, Osage Co., Okla. *Underside*, winter form 9/22/96, Tallgrass Prairie Preserve, Osage Co., Okla. *Upperside*, summer form 8/14/99, Pontotoc Preserve, Pontotoc Co., Okla. *Underside*, summer form 6/16/01, Pontotoc Preserve, Pontotoc Co., Okla.

Eastern Comma: *Upperside*, summer form 5/19/02, Oxley Nature Center, Tulsa Co., Okla. *Underside*, summer form 6/10/01, Pontotoc Preserve, Pontotoc Co., Okla.

Mourning Cloak: *Upperside*, 5/31/99, Lincoln Co., Okla. (auto casualty), **J. Dole**. *Underside*, 10/6/96, Tallgrass Prairie Preserve, Osage Co., Okla.

American Lady: *Upperside*, 6/6/01, Pontotoc Preserve, Pontotoc Co., Okla. *Underside*, 8/1/97, Tallgrass Prairie Preserve, Osage Co., Okla.

Painted Lady: *Upperside*, 10/27/99, Santa Anna National Wildlife Refuge, Hildago Co., Tex. *Underside*, 8/16/99, Tulsa, Tulsa Co., Okla.

Red Admiral: *Upperside*, 10/11/98, Tallgrass Prairie Preserve, Osage Co., Okla. *Underside*, 6/26/99, Ottawa Co., Okla.

Common Buckeye: *Upperside*, 7/26/01, Tulsa Garden Center, Tulsa Co., Okla. *Underside*, summer form 9/3/00, Oxley Nature Center, Tulsa Co., Okla.

Red-spotted Purple: *Upperside*, 8/14/99, Pontotoc Preserve, Pontotoc

Co., Okla. *Underside*, 8/14/99, Pontotoc Preserve, Pontotoc Co., Okla.

Viceroy: *Upperside*, 8/14/99, Pontotoc Preserve, Pontotoc Co., Okla. *Underside*, 8/22/99, Sanborn Lake, Payne Co., Okla., **J. Dole**.

Common Mestra: *Upperside*, 10/21/99, Santa Anna National Wildlife Refuge, Hidalgo Co., Tex. *Underside*, 10/21/99, Santa Anna National Wildlife Refuge, Hidalgo Co., Tex.

Goatweed Leafwing: *Upperside*, male winter form 10/24/96, Tallgrass Prairie Preserve, Osage Co., Okla. *Underside*, male winter form 10/6/96, Tallgrass Prairie Preserve, Osage Co., Okla.

Hackberry Emperor: *Upperside*, 7/11/99, Pontotoc Preserve, Pontotoc Co., Okla. *Underside*, 5/15/01, Oxley Nature Center, Tulsa Co., Okla.

Tawny Emperor: *Upperside*, 6/6/00, Pontotoc Preserve, Pontotoc Co., Okla. *Underside*, 10/21/99, Santa Anna National Wildlife Refuge, Hildago Co., Tex.

Northern Pearly-eye: *Underside*, 5/28/00, Ottawa Co., Okla.

Gemmed Satyr: *Underside*, 10/24/99, near Roma, Starr Co., Tex.

Carolina Satyr: *Underside*, 6/6/00, Pontotoc Preserve, Pontotoc Co., Okla.

Little Wood-Satyr: *Upperside*, 7/3/99, Tallgrass Prairie Preserve, Osage Co., Okla., **J. Dole**. *Underside*, 6/11/99, Pontotoc Preserve, Pontotoc Co., Okla.

Common Wood-Nymph: *Underside*, yellow form 7/15/97, Tallgrass Prairie Preserve, Osage Co., Okla. *Underside*, dark form 9/5/98, Lake Etling State Park, Cimarron Co., Okla., **J. Dole**.

Monarch: *Upperside*, male 9/27/97, Tallgrass Prairie Preserve, Osage Co., Okla. *Upperside*, female 9/27/97, Tallgrass Prairie Preserve, Osage Co., Okla. *Underside*, 8/29/99, Stillwater, Payne Co., Okla.

Queen: *Upperside*, 6/15/00, Pontotoc Preserve, Pontotoc Co., Okla. *Underside*, 6/15/00, Pontotoc Preserve, Pontotoc Co., Okla.

Silver-spotted Skipper: *Upperside*, 10/30/00, Tulsa Garden Center, Tulsa Co., Okla. *Underside*, 10/30/00, Tulsa Garden Center, Tulsa Co., Okla.

Hoary Edge: *Upperside*, 5/14/00, Pontotoc Preserve, Pontotoc Co.,

Okla. *Underside*, 5/14/00, Pontotoc Preserve, Pontotoc Co., Okla.

Southern Cloudywing: *Upperside*, 6/22/00, Tallgrass Prairie Preserve, Osage Co., Okla. *Underside*, 8/22/99, Stillwater, Payne Co., Okla.

Northern Cloudywing: *Upperside*, 7/15/97, Tallgrass Prairie Preserve, Osage Co., Okla. *Underside*, 5/14/00, Pontotoc Preserve, Pontotoc Co., Okla.

Hayhurst's Scallopwing: *Upperside*, male 6/18/98, Cucumber Creek, LeFlore Co., Okla. *Upperside*, female 8/29/99, Stillwater, Payne Co., Okla.

Horace's Duskywing: *Upperside*, male 7/28/96, Tallgrass Prairie Preserve, Osage Co., Okla. *Upperside*, female 6/18/98, Cucumber Creek, LeFlore Co., Okla. *Underside*, 7/23/99, Tulsa, Tulsa Co., Okla.

Funereal Duskywing: *Upperside*, 10/21/99, Santa Anna National Wildlife Refuge, Hidalgo Co., Tex. *Underside*, 6/15/00, Pontotoc Preserve, Pontotoc Co., Okla.

Wild Indigo Duskywing: *Upperside*, male 7/11/99, Pontotoc Preserve, Pontotoc Co., Okla. *Upperside*, female 6/14/99, Pontotoc Preserve, Pontotoc Co., Okla. *Underside*, 7/11/99, Pontotoc Preserve, Pontotoc Co., Okla.

Common Checkered-Skipper: *Upperside*, male 12/1/98, Tulsa, Tulsa Co., Okla. *Upperside*, female 10/22/99, Mission, Hidalgo Co., Tex. *Underside*, 9/1/96, Tallgrass Prairie Preserve, Osage Co., Okla.

Common Sootywing: *Upperside*, male 8/22/99, Stillwater, Payne Co., Okla. *Upperside*, female 8/22/99, Stillwater, Payne Co., Okla.

Clouded Skipper: *Upperside*, male 10/224/99, near Roma, Starr Co., Tex. *Upperside*, female 9/14/99, Tulsa, Tulsa Co., Okla. *Underside*, 9/14/99, Tulsa, Tulsa Co., Okla.

Least Skipper: *Upperside*, 7/24/99, Tallgrass Prairie Preserve, Osage Co., Okla. *Underside*, 7/24/99, Tallgrass Prairie Preserve, Osage Co., Okla.

Fiery Skipper: *Upperside*, male 12/1/98, Tulsa Garden Center, Tulsa Co., Okla. *Underside*, male 7/24/99, Tallgrass Prairie Preserve,

Osage Co., Okla. *Upperside*, female 7/5/99, Tulsa, Tulsa Co., Okla. *Underside*, female 12/1/98, Tulsa Garden Center, Tulsa Co., Okla.

Green Skipper: *Upperside*, male 5/14/00, Pontotoc Preserve, Pontotoc Co., Okla. *Underside*, 5/14/00, Pontotoc Preserve, Pontotoc Co., Okla.

Dotted Skipper: *Upperside*, female 6/6/00 Pontotoc Preserve, Pontotoc Co., Okla. *Underside*, 6/6/00, Pontotoc Preserve, Pontotoc Co., Okla.

Tawny-edged Skipper: *Upperside*, male 6/6/00, Pontotoc Preserve, Pontotoc Co., Okla. *Upperside*, female 9/21/00, Pawhuska, Osage Co., Okla. *Underside*, 7/25/97, Tallgrass Prairie Preserve, Osage Co., Okla.

Crossline Skipper: *Upperside*, male 6/12/90, Copan Lake, Washington Co., Okla. (pinned specimen collected by J. Nelson). *Underside*, 5/14/00, Pontotoc Preserve, Pontotoc Co., Okla.

Southern Broken-Dash: *Upperside*, male 8/22/99, Stillwater, Payne Co., Okla. *Upperside*, female 6/10/01, Nickel Preserve, Cherokee Co., Okla. *Underside*, 9/9/00, Oxley Nature Center, Tulsa Co., Okla.

Sachem: *Upperside*, male 10/30/00, Tulsa Garden Center, Tulsa Co., Okla. *Underside*, male 10/13/00, Tulsa, Tulsa Co., Okla. *Upperside*, female 10/30/00, Tulsa Garden Center, Tulsa Co., Okla. *Underside*, female 7/24/99, Tallgrass Prairie Preserve, Osage Co., Okla.

Arogos Skipper: *Underside*, 6/6/00, Pontotoc Preserve, Pontotoc Co., Okla.

Delaware Skipper: *Upperside*, male 4/26/96, Tallgrass Prairie Preserve, Osage Co., Okla. *Upperside*, female 8/22/99, Stillwater, Payne Co., Okla., **J. Dole**. *Underside*, 7/30/01, Tulsa, Tulsa Co., Okla.

Zabulon Skipper: *Upperside*, male 4/27/00, Tulsa, Tulsa Co., Okla. *Underside*, male 8/29/99, Stillwater, Payne Co., Okla. *Upperside*, female 8/1/97, Tallgrass Prairie Preserve, Osage Co., Okla. *Underside*, female 8/1/97, Tallgrass Prairie Preserve, Osage Co., Okla.

Dun Skipper: *Upperside*, male 6/6/00, Pontotoc Preserve, Pontotoc Co., Okla. *Underside*, male 7/30/01, Tulsa, Tulsa Co., Okla. *Upperside*, female 6/19/00, Tulsa, Tulsa Co., Okla. *Underside*, female 8/1/97, Tallgrass Prairie Preserve, Osage Co., Okla.

Nysa Roadside-Skipper: *Upperside*, 10/22/99, Yturria Brush Tract, Hidalgo Co., Tex. *Underside*, 9/21/00, Pawhuska, Osage Co., Okla.

Common Roadside-Skipper: *Upperside*, 4/15/01, Oxley Nature Center, Tulsa Co., Okla. *Underside*, 8/22/99, Stillwater, Payne Co., Okla.

Bell's Roadside-Skipper: *Upperside*, 8/16/99, Tulsa, Tulsa Co., Okla. *Underside*, 8/11/99, Tulsa, Tulsa Co., Okla.

Eufala Skipper: *Upperside*, 7/24/00, Pontotoc Preserve, Pontotoc Co., Okla. *Underside*, 8/14/99, Pontotoc Preserve, Pontotoc Co., Okla.

Ocola Skipper: *Underside*, 10/21/99, Santa Anna National Wildlife Refuge, Hidalgo Co., Tex.

Yucca Giant-Skipper: *Upperside*, 4/12/01, Weymouth Woods, Moore Co., N.C., **J. Dole**. *Underside*, 4/12/01, Weymouth Woods, Moore Co., N.C., **J. Dole**.

Fig. 1.1: 3/27/00, Tulsa Co., Okla.

Fig. 1.2: 7/3/99, Tulsa Co., Okla.

Fig. 1.3: 10/2/99, Tulsa Co., Okla.

Fig. 1.4: 5/23/00, Tulsa Co., Okla.

Fig. 1.5: 9/27/97, Tallgrass Prairie Preserve, Osage Co., Okla.

Fig. 2.1: 8/29/99, Stillwater, Payne Co., Okla.

Fig. 2.2: 6/16/01, Pontotoc Preserve, Pontotoc Co., Okla.

Fig. 3.1: 8/1/97, Tallgrass Prairie Preserve, Osage Co., Okla.

Fig. 3.2: 7/28/98, Tulsa Co., Okla.

Fig. 3.3: 7/11/99, Pontotoc Preserve, Pontotoc Co., Okla.

Fig. 3.4: 9/23/99, Stillwater, Payne Co., Okla., **J. Dole**.

Index

*Numbers in **bold** after butterfly names refer to the pages of the main species accounts.*